12/93

Dear Kathy,

Hope you enjoy! Thought you might get some ideas for your flower arrangements for John & Toni's wedding!

Love & Merry Christmas,
Lorraine

COUNTRY STYLE

FLOWERS

COUNTRY STYLE
FLOWERS

FIONNA HILL

PHOTOGRAPHY
NICHOLAS TRESIDDER

CRESCENT BOOKS
NEW YORK • AVENEL, NEW JERSEY

For my mother Eve and
my friend Gary

This 1993 edition published by Crescent Books,
distributed by Outlet Book Company, Inc., a Random House Company,
40 Engelhard Avenue, Avenel, New Jersey 07001

Random House
New York • Toronto • London • Sydney • Auckland

First Published 1992
Reprinted in 1993

Publisher: Robin Burgess
Publishing Coordinator: Donna Hoyle
Art Direction, Styling and Design: Donna Hoyle
Photography: Nicholas Tresidder
Editor: Diana Harris

Typeset in New Zealand by Jazz Graphics.
Finished artwork by Michelle Tack and Justin Wishart, Donna Hoyle Design Ltd.
Printed in Singapore by Imago.

Country Flowers
ISBN: 0 517 10334 6

ABOVE

An antique cider funnel with a bucket lining
has lots of character for a 'no flower' arrangement.
Branches from quince (Cydonia oblonga), pear and apple trees,
all bearing fruit, form the boldest materials. Rose hips, alder
cones, barberry and grapes add other berries and textures, and
an abandoned bird's nest is snuggled in near the centre.

A *huge Italian terracotta saucer makes a wonderful centrepiece
for a special occasion, but it needs a lot of space.
Ornamental pumpkins and gourds form the largest items,* Idesia
polycarpa *berries tumble over the sides, and pots of planted
parsley add a fresh green, as do privet berries, The other materials
are beetroot,* Pyracantha *berries, ornamental kale* (Brassica
oleracea acephala), *dried maize, and a single pomegranate.*

CONTENTS

INTRODUCTION

IN THE LAST FEW YEARS, NEW attitudes to the way we live have developed. Many people have taken to leading more healthy, active lives; they appreciate natural foods, fabrics, and simple country articles. Their lives may be busier, but they are more casual, too, and the environment has assumed a greater importance for them. Consequently, cottage-style gardens and plants are now popular, and a freer, natural look has developed in flowers.

The current fashion for collecting 'country' crafts lends itself to country-style flower arrangements; simple, unpretentious containers provide an air of warmth and informality and a sense of comfort. It is also fun to use rustic containers that are not normally thought of as vases — old tin baths, washing bowls, wooden barrels, old baskets, and even chamber pots.

Flowers are an important part of interior design. Together with other natural materials, they can bring a room to life, and make it look lived in. They are also the most renewable and least expensive way to enliven an interior.

I have always been interested in nature, flowers and beautiful things. It was from my mother that I learnt to appreciate gardens; she had 'green fingers', and was a keen and knowledgeable gardener of both flowers and vegetables. My father tended to come along later for follow-up work, but this was not always welcome. As a young child I acted as a spy for my mother when dad ventured too near her precious plants with his hoe in hand. His domain was a prolific greenhouse for tomatoes, cucumbers and grapes.

My mother was an adventurous gardener with an eye for the unusual — no rows of bedding plants of garishly contrasting colours for her. I recall her surreptitiously bringing home (in a money belt around her waist) from an overseas trip, seeds from Switzerland, and subsequently experimenting with gentians and edelweiss.

My mother and I picked the flowers from her garden and she encouraged me to arrange them. She bought remnants of fabric in sales and, as a child, I used to hang them from a pelmet in our hallway to create settings against which my flower arrangements were placed on a small table.

Once, when we were on holiday at our cottage by a river, I remember my brother and I taking buckets and cutting off thousands of the flower-heads of wild, lemon-yellow lupins. We then set off in our dinghy and rowed to the centre of the slow-flowing river and emptied the flowers overboard to create a pale yellow, moving mass. It dispersed all too quickly and was rather destructive and wasteful, but it made a wonderful spectacle.

While I was living in England, I attended the famous Constance Spry Flower School in London. After gaining my diploma, I was fortunate to be offered a job in one of Constance Spry's London flower shops.

Constance Spry believed that cut flowers should be handled in a natural, free-flowing, countrified way that recalled, rather than denied, how they had looked in the garden. Staid, triangular arrangements with bows springing out of them were not her style: I had found a fellow spirit.

Her philosophy was not rule-bound. She said, 'Never forget that in arranging flowers you have the opportunity to express your own sense of what is beautiful and you should feel free and uninhibited in doing so.'

I recall, as a student at the Flower School, seeing a bouquet being made by one of the teachers. It was to be presented to the Queen Mother, on the opening night of Shakespeare's *As You Like It*. There was not a flower in sight: instead, a posy made of all the English hedgerow items mentioned in the play, like herbs, hawthorn and oak-apples.

The warm tones in this screen are echoed in a dried Christmas arrangement. Dried sphagnum moss lines the old wire basket and holds dry floral foam. The materials include a preserved, holly-like foliage, a variety of cones, and man-made berries and apples. An artificial robin peeps through the branches.

FACING PAGE

*A pine dresser base, backed by pictures of boldly illustrated vegetables and fruit, is the kitchen setting for this glowing arrangement of Iceland poppies (*Papaver nudicaule) *and lime-green* Euphorbia robbiae, *to disguise the mechanics. (Poppies also look wonderful in a setting with light coming from behind them.)*

Constance Spry was an innovator with an eye for the unusual and unexpected; never before had anyone dared to use wild grasses, berries and even cow parsley in arrangements, until she introduced them. She was the first to combine glasshouse with garden or wild flowers, and also the first to use kale (the humble cabbage) with flowers.

My time at the Constance Spry shop gave me an entrée into a world that I otherwise would not have known. I helped to do flowers for society weddings in the beautiful St. Margaret's Chapel that adjoins Westminster Abbey, in the historic Inigo Jones designed Lincoln's Inn Chapel, and in the Guards Chapel. Another interesting experience involved doing flowers for a charity ball in Madame Tussaud's waxworks, setting arrangements amongst many famous faces.

Since my days at Constance Spry I have developed my own style and have become much more adventurous, moving from classic to contemporary styles, using eclectic mixtures of materials, such as vegetables, weeds and wildflowers combined with conventional flowers.

Mosses have wonderful, subtle colours and textures and bring the earthy forest floor indoors. I also love rustic materials like lichen, cones and birds' nests. My fascination has led me to make my own nests, and I now weave authentic-looking copies from horse fodder, stitched together with a sack needle and raffia. I decorate the tops with moss, lichen and feathers.

<hr>

ABOVE

This bath-shaped grey tin is a good holder for white flowers and grey foliages. It has been wired to hold the flowers which include Cosmos bipinnatus, *Lisianthus, Queen Anne's lace and the curious green rose,* Rosa chinensis 'Viridiflora'.

Shapes and colours of vegetables and fruit, berries, seeds and nuts are a great source of inspiration. Globe artichokes are beautifully formed, often with hints of purple, and their leaves are a soft silver-grey. Aubergines are rich and glossy. Beetroot have vibrant red stems and interesting, veined leaves.

Many vegetables and herbs — such as parsnips, carrots, parsley, fennel and leeks — if they are allowed to go to seed, have lovely seed heads.

I have created a stunning arrangement with bright yellow tulips and the leaves of glossy, dark green silver beet. I've combined exotic orchids with berries, swedes, turnips and moss. Gourds, pumpkins and maize engender an atmosphere of harvest time, while apples, oranges and pineapples look great in a Christmas creation.

Foliage alone can make an interesting arrangement — mixed greenery, with perhaps a few berries, gives a lovely country look.

Many people live in cities, often without a garden or even a glimpse of greenery. A country-style flower arrangement is a means of putting them back in touch with nature, and it brings a fresh breath of the country into busy urban lives.

Flowers are as important an accessory as ornaments, paintings and books, and more people are including them as part of their regular shopping list. They should not be brought out just for special occasions — flowers should be part of our everyday lives.

RIGHT

I have taken a rustic moss basket and glued dried camellias around its rim, and wound additional moss amongst the blooms.
The basket is lined with plastic and extravagantly heaped with dried rose buds and their leaves. A peony is placed in the centre and a few blue hydrangea flowers and the fine baby-blue ribbon, entwined around the handle, echo the blue in the rich tapestry fabric.

CHAPTER ONE

NATURE'S BOUNTY

You'll never lack supplies from Nature's hands,
if you're content with what your need demands.
Cato

THE EASIEST WAY TO ACHIEVE A country-style look is by making use of the natural materials in the world around you.

Learn to develop an eye for interesting items. When you are out walking or driving, be observant and try to picture things out of their environment. Envisage them in your home with other materials and accessories, bearing in mind your own containers and the colours of your decor. Be adventurous, and don't limit your options by ignoring so-called 'weeds'.

Plants that grow completely naturally have all the idiosyncrasies that are normally bred out of commercially grown flowers; the quirks of nature are what give them their charm.

Vegetables, fruit and seeds are another source of inspiration. They bring another dimension to an arrangement, either in combination with flowers, or foliage, or both, and they have the impact of the unexpected.

I love mosses, lichens and fungus. They have a mysterious quality — a special eeriness that I find very attractive — and they come in such subtle, restrained colours.

I am constantly on the look-out for bits and pieces, and even in the large city where I live, there are treasures to be found. Derelict buildings and sites often have ivy climbing over them, sometimes the old plants with dusky black berries and unusual leaf growth. And ivy has the added attraction of being a traditional, noble plant with symbolic importance. In mythology it was sacred to Bacchus, the god of wine, and it has an historic link to festivals and merriment.

FACING PAGE

A bird's eye view of some of nature's green
and white bounty: foliage, cones, fruit,
berries, moss, vegetables, seed pods
and flowers.

Along the roadsides I watch out for grasses, in their green state or later, when they have seeded and dried. Wild flowers are lovely, too. Many do not last well in water once they are picked, but they make a charming, short-lived arrangement. If you think you may be in a place where you can pick wild flowers and weeds, take along a polythene bag with damp newspaper in the bottom. Place the cut flowers in it, blow it up slightly so that the bag does not collapse on the flowers, and seal it with a tie. As soon as possible, get them treated and into water, in a cool environment. Don't leave them in a hot car for too long.

Whenever I fly home to visit my family I return with new finds. My sister's garage always has some special treasures waiting for me: onion flowers, poppy seeds and pussy willow hang from the rafters, cones are drying on paper on the floor, and there are branches off a fallen tree, and birds' nests. I have more time to forage for materials there, and the different climate produces a new selection of goodies. I return home with unusual-looking, bulging packages; on one occasion with one beginning to seep elderberry juice from a paper rubbish sack, looking a bit like a body in a bag!

Prunings can be a wonderful resource. The soft tips of bare birch stems, before the leaves have formed, can be used for many things. They can be twisted into wreaths, wound around basket handles and rims, or tied into bows and other shapes and then dried for use later. (See the birch bow on page 141). Birch branches and trunks make attractive stems for topiaries, with their lovely silver-grey patches and interesting texture. Many of the trunks I use for topiary come from the firewood pile: interesting lengths of wood, sometimes with cones attached.

FACING PAGE

A collection of mosses, lichens, fungi and pumice waits to be used.

The Lenten Hellebore Helleborus orientalis.

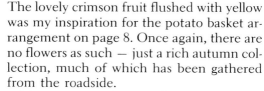

The bold form of Bergenia cordifolia.

The lovely apple-green Helleborus corsicus.

Look out also for branches and trunks of trees covered with fascinating lichen, and for sculptural shapes: character-filled, gnarled branches (living or dead) have many uses and can be stored away for later use. They can also be employed again and again for different purposes. There can also be an added bonus; bare branches from a tree like the horse chestnut will open later in water. If you pick the branches just before the spring growth appears, their bulbous, sticky buds will burst forth into fresh, green shoots.

Branches from fruit trees with blossom or fruit on them look lovely in an arrangement. Of course, they have to be able to be spared; I wouldn't raid a tree unless there were branches which needed cutting off. The outline and main component of the arrangement on page 33 is blossom from a friend's old pear tree which needed pruning.

Look at the materials in the old cider funnel on page 5. There are no flowers, just a bountiful mix of fruit, hips, cones and a favourite (abandoned) bird's nest. Quinces are amongst my favourite fruits, and the trees live to a ripe old age so they are usually full of character. The blossom is perfect and the fruit is beautiful, with a fine fur on it.

Another friend wanted to cut some side branches from her Jack Humm crab-apple.

The lovely crimson fruit flushed with yellow was my inspiration for the potato basket arrangement on page 8. Once again, there are no flowers as such — just a rich autumn collection, much of which has been gathered from the roadside.

I live near a railway track and find many treasures along the line: bright nasturtiums, a type of marrow with mottled, green skin, watercress in a stream near the line, and wild fennel, the flowers and seeds of which are lovely at all stages of growth. There is also a cool, damp bank with maidenhair fern and moss growing on it, along with weeds, such as buttercups and plantain, and blackberries, too — if I find them before the birds do.

After a trip to a lake bordered by a forest, I drove home with my car loaded up with most of the items that you see in the photograph on page 16. A large branch, covered in fungus, had fallen off a dead tree. There was pale green lichen, which hangs from tree branches like an old man's beard, fresh, green moss lifted from the ground, and a ghostly, soft, creamish/grey moss, also from the ground (it is crisp when it dries and has a form that looks like miniature coral). I found a lichen growing on the trunks of willow trees and another, in greens and greys, which looks like tiny reindeer antlers. I gathered up pale,

greyish white pumice from the lake's edge (it was a volcanic area). To top it off, I found a large bush of pink flowering currant growing beside a river, and I picked some branches, filling my car with their fresh, tangy perfume.

But it is important not to abuse nature's bounty. Be careful when cutting plants that are growing wild. Do not destroy them, be aware of those which are protected species, and observe the rules applying to reserves, parks and private land. In some countries laws forbid the importation of seeds and other vegetable matter.

The collections of flowers, foliage and other materials on the following pages are my choice of materials for the different colour groupings. They reflect a season — early autumn — so there are naturally omissions because they have all been gathered at one time. Conversely, some of the flowers are commercially grown and not normally associated with autumn, like the freesias and irises.

A pyramid of rich purple berries, seeds and fruit. The tazza matches the china of the French fruit set and the fruit picks up some of the colours of the purple fruit on the china (see page 162 for instructions).

Because these collections reflect my preferences in colour, there is a predominance of green and white. The combination is restful to look at and makes you feel that nature has come indoors. I wish green flowers were much more widely available commercially, and not regarded as curiosities.

Euphorbias and hellebores are among my favourites. I love the acid-green of many of the euphorbias and the lime-green *Helleborus corsicus* is special. When arranging them, I try to position the clusters in such a way that you can see into the perfect flowers. Green hydrangeas often have a soft pink blush, nicotiana is a fresh lime-green and alchemilla is a soft yellow-green. Alchemilla has a beautifully shaped leaf too, with a soft bloom on it.

Foliage of some kind is available all year round. Use leaves for their singular beauty; you don't always have to have flowers. A huge jug of *Magnolia grandiflora* or copper beech leaves looks great in a large space. Or you can arrange a mixture of greenery in different shapes and shades, and imitate nature.

Of course, foliage isn't always green — there are many wonderful hues and even more shapes and textures. Variegated leaves add variety, and autumn brings its own treasure trove.

Green vegetables, fruit berries and seed pods add another dimension. The creeper *Araujia sericifera*, in the green photograph, is regarded as a pest and treated with disdain. But, taken out of their usual environment and clustered into the centre of an arrangement, its large pods look most interesting.

Most common garden flowers have a white form. The textures of and markings on white flowers produce great variety, so that even in a monochrome arrangement you can achieve diversity because of this. I love the green markings on snowdrops, or the tips of some white delphiniums.

I prefer not to mix white flowers with other coloured flowers, combining them instead with interesting greenery. And nothing is more beautiful than a mass of white anemones or *Helleborus niger.*

Anemone coronaria 'The Bride'

I am also fond of blue flowers, especially the true blue ones like cornflowers. The soft blue of tweedia and plumbago is lovely, too. And the Himalayan blue poppy (*Meconopsis betonicifolia*) is to me one of the most beautiful of all flowers. There are many variations of blue, even within the one family — like the delicate shades of delphiniums.

Blue and purple flowers, although lovely, are a receding colour. They can be a little lost against some backgrounds and do not show up well under artificial light. Take care when using blue in a large mixed arrangement that will be seen from a distance; the blue flowers may look like dark holes in the arrangement.

In the blue picture selection I have also incorporated purple and pink. Bright pink flowers are not my favourites (although I like dusky pink and apricot flowers). White

peonies are superb, but I find pink ones a little blowsy — except, perhaps, the palest form.

Fruit like grapes and plums, and vegetables such as aubergine, red cabbage and ornamental kale go well with grey foliages. I included most of them in the white picture, but these leaves also look lovely with blue, purple and pink flowers, especially the 'muddy' colours that appeal to me.

ABOVE

A *mottled grey enamel bowl holds tulips,* Alstroemeria, *anemones, grapes, guavas, aubergines, privet berries, and the first crocuses. The foliage includes* Stachys byzantina, Cerinthe retorta, Helichrysum petiolatum, *ornamental kale* (Brassica oleracea acephala), *and the black seeds are* Aristea ecklonii.

Red is the vital colour of fire, passion and life. In the right setting I love to mix clashing reds boldly, but I need to get the proportions of the different reds just right. The fruit and vegetable world has some wonderful red specimens, and brown cones and nuts look lovely with these mixtures.

ABOVE

A rustic wooden barrel lined with a wired plastic bucket.
The interesting bare red branches are maple, the flowers are asiatic lilies, spray chrysanthemums and brown boronia (Boronia megastigma).
The foliage is angelica, copper beech, magnolia and branches of ripe mandarins.

The last of the colour collections is a vibrant mixture of yellow and orange. It has the feeling of both spring and autumn; yellow is the colour of spring, and orange carries a feeling of autumn, mainly because the orange component consists of gourds, pumpkins, berries, vegetables and fruit.

The arranged basket above contains much of the same mixture and also invokes the wholesome atmosphere of the harvest. A willow basket from Burgundy is lined with straw and filled with *Pyracantha* berries, sunflowers, *Boltonia, Alstroemeria,* freesias, and other interesting bits and pieces. *Idesia polycarpa* berries and yellow courgettes spill over the front.

I hope that reading this chapter has fired your imagination and opened your eyes to the wider possibilities that surround you in the natural world. It is here that you will find the many materials that can be combined into unusual and exciting arrangements to enhance your home.

CHAPTER TWO

INTERIORS

*A detail of the centre of the grape basket
showing its wide handle.*

ONCE YOU HAVE GATHERED YOUR components together, you need to make sure they are used to best effect.

Country-style decor suits a casual, abundant look in arrangements. Even if you have just a few flowers, a generous appearance can be achieved with the addition of foliage, seeds, berries and branches, enhanced by the use of simple, functional containers.

In a country-style setting, try to ensure that the flowers are suitable. For example, lilies in an urn would probably look too grand — unless, of course, they were for a special occasion.

Some rooms, because of their scale, require large arrangements, but there are also many situations that call for small, simple items, and others where you can create a 'still life' by grouping interesting containers with simple country mixtures, and using a colour theme.

If you wish to accentuate a particular feature or accessory in a room, place your flowers near it. For example, you may wish to highlight a colourful sampler, so arrange flowers in toning hues on a table to the side of, or in front of it. Familiar patterns can take on a new life when complemented by flowers.

FACING PAGE

*The antique, wooden grape-picker's basket
holds an exuberant autumn display.
The mixture includes* Nandina domestica
'Nana' *and* Virginia creeper (Parthenocissus
inserta) *leaves, deep-red spray
chrysanthemums and green and red hydrangea
flowers, and the berries are rose hips, rowan*
(Sorbus aucuparia), *Pyracantha,* Clivia
miniata, *dogwood* (Cornus capitata), *Jack
Humm crab-apples, and tiny cocktail tomatoes.*

ENTRANCES

The entrance is an important part of the house, because this is the point of arrival and it sets the scene for the rest of the house. It is also the place where farewells are made and again, impressions linger.

Perfumed flowers at an entrance are a wonderful greeting for guests.

Sometimes an entrance hall area, because comparatively little time is spent there, can be decorated in a more visually stimulating way than the rest of the house, and therefore you can be more dramatic with flowers than you might be elsewhere. Some of the flower-arranging rules can be broken for a display in a hall for this reason. You could do a huge, 'over the top' display, which might impede vision in another part of the house, or take up too much 'living' space elsewhere.

Most country-style entrances are likely to have a homely appearance and may house a clutter of hats, coats, umbrellas and boots. These items can be gathered together attractively and accompanied by a bold arrangement (see page 35), or the entrance may have a feature like an impressive painting or a piece of furniture that can also be enhanced by flowers (see facing page).

An entrance with stairs can provide interesting spaces like alcoves, window ledges and shelves in which to set flowers, and on special occasions, like Christmas or a wedding, bannisters can be attractively decorated (see page 98).

Sometimes a hallway is dark, with very little natural light, in which case it would be a suitable spot for a dried flower display. Hallways may also be small areas, where you could consider hanging wall drops or wreaths. And a wreath on the door is a welcoming sign for guests before they step indoors.

The outside of a door can be decorated in other ways. For a special occasion you could surround the top and sides of a door frame with fresh materials instead of dried, as shown on page 141.

ABOVE

This sturdy metal basket is lined with lichen and a wired plastic bowl. The green materials are bells of Ireland (Molucella laevis), three euphorbias — marginata, epithymoides, and amygdaloides — Alchemilla mollis and hosta.

FACING PAGE

A front door opens on to a Georgian pine dresser base. The container is a Victorian wire rubbish basket, closely lined with lichen and holding a wired plastic bucket. Apart from pear tree branches, the other flowers here are bells of Ireland (Molucella laevis), white broom, Spiraea cantoniensis, Helleborus corsicus, unripened loquats, pussy willow and Stachyurus praecox.

FACING PAGE

FACING PAGE

This entrance hall has a large wooden table enhanced by an antique, mustard-coloured cache-pot. As the cache-pot has a hole in the bottom, it is lined with a wired plastic bucket.
Magnolia grandiflora *leaves make a strong background, and the flowers are shasta daisies,* Longiflorum *lilies,* Euphorbia *species,* Nigella *seeds and fennel seeds.*

RIGHT

An old jug holds a generous mass of Solidaster luteus *(a cross between golden rod and aster) and a few wild grass seeds. The jug doesn't need wiring; it has a narrow neck and the stems with their profuse tops of flowers fall in a pleasing way by themselves, giving a very natural, uncontrived look.*

LIVING ROOMS

Whether the room is bright and spacious, or intimate and cosy, a living room will benefit from flowers. However, make sure that your decoration is in scale with its surroundings — the furniture, the wallpaper and fabric patterns, and the accessories — and try to choose flowers that are sympathetic to them.

A good place to put flowers is on a side table that is used mostly for display purposes, and where the flowers will not be in the way. The table may have a lamp, to provide soft light from above, which is very flattering to flowers.

Use coffee tables for flowers only if they are uncrowded; a coffee table is often a working place, for newspapers, books and suchlike, rather than a decorative point in a room.

Do not put fresh flowers on a television set, in case water is spilt on it. Dried flowers would be more suitable here.

Flowers are best viewed at eye level or below, so try not to place them too high.

RIGHT

The interiors shown in this and the following three pictures are good examples of country decor. The flowers here complement the natural materials and soft tones of their surroundings.
A large dresser displaying a mixture of china is the busy background for a tin bowl of sunny yellow and white flowers.
The flowers include spray chrysanthemums, gerberas, 'Iceberg' roses, larkspur and camellias and the berries are unripe privet.

FACING PAGE

A blue-painted living room filled with interesting items. The small galvanised-tin bath is wired and holds a mixture of blue flowers and grey foliage including irises, delphiniums, gentian and salvia.

slow and progress gradually. The important thing is to get started, and maintain your plan.

3. Identify your barriers to exercise. If you identify an obstacle, challenge yourself to come up with a plan to get around it. If you find exercise boring, you might identify friends or family members you can invite to exercise with you.

4. Devise a plan. Research shows that people are more likely to stay active if they set up reasonable measurable goals, come up with a set schedule, and keep a written log of their progress.

If you are lucky enough to have a fireplace in your living room, it will probably be the focus of the room. A mantelpiece is a good place for flowers, but don't allow them to protrude too far into the room. In summer, the fireplace itself makes a good recess for a flower arrangement (see page 135).

If you put flowers in front of a mirror, make sure the mechanics at the back are not reflected. Disguise the wire with foliage.

LEFT

An old and battered blue enamel billy holds a pretty blue garden mixture: plumbago, lavender, gentian, forget-me-not, and tweedia.

FACING PAGE

The wooden dresser in this family room holds a collection of china, the yellow colour of which is echoed in this casual grouping of flowers.
The basket is lined with a wired plastic bowl. Sunlight catches the glowing colours of the flowers, which are Boltonia, bells of Ireland (Molucella laevis), antirrhinum, 'Belladonna' delphiniums, asters and amaranthus.
On the floor, a basket filled with ornamental gourds carries on the yellow theme.

This wooden-slatted basket is lined with
straw and holds a wired plastic container.
The flowers are butter-yellow gerbera,
achillea, white feverfew and Scotch briar
rose hips. The unusual seed heads are those
of Echinacea purpurea.

ABOVE

Old roses in soft tones of cream, lemon and
pink are casually massed in an old tin
dipper, with mesh inside it. The roses
include 'Sombreuil', 'Moonlight' and pale
lemon 'Mermaid' with some of its branches
showing persistent stamens on
developing heps.

L

This charming paint
pretty background f
pastel colours si
painting. The dou
sweet peas, roses
mollis, Scotch briar
garden bits and
coloured roses
'Na

*Don't have access to the internet? Try your local library or senior center.

FACING PAGE

This large arrangement, created for a special
occasion, is one of a pair set in alcoves on
either side of a fireplace in a living room.
It is set in a large, wired, green ceramic
container and the mid-summer flowers are
hydrangeas, delphiniums, trachelium, irises,
wallflowers, sweet-william, godetia and
wild carrot.

ABOVE

A round, galvanised-tin pan holds a rich mixture of red and green parrot tulips and cerise tulips. The foliage includes the pink and green leaves of ornamental kale (Brassica oleracea acephala) *and the grey leaves of* Helichrysum petiolatum *and* Senecio cineraria.

FACING PAGE

This painting inspired an almost all-green arrangement that included some unusual materials. Three leek flowers rise high at the back, there are seeds and some leaves of angelica, parsley and Canna indica, *and the flowers and leaves of acanthus.*
The acanthus leaves form a striking background for the aubergines and artichokes that make up the focal point.

ABOVE

*An antique chamber pot patterned with
hops makes an unexpected container for this
cool mixture. The yellowy green of*
Euphorbia robbiae *contrasts with blue
tweedia, delphiniums, and scillas.
Bells of Ireland* (Molucella laevis) *add
a touch of fresh green.*

The true green Ixia viridiflora, *with its dark eye, looks almost unreal. The bunches are casually arranged in a trio of old green bottles.*
The plates are hand-painted, with centres depicting individual flowers.

RIGHT

A spongeware china jug is a suitably simple container for a bunch of sweet peas.

FACING PAGE

A butcher's block makes a base for this large arrangement. An old wired bucket holds the full-blown summer mixture which includes hydrangeas, delphiniums, astilbe, Canterbury bells, and the rich leaves of copper beech. There are also three plastic cones on sticks hidden at different points, to enable the peonies to be arranged high in the display and not just at the bottom. (Don't forget to top the cones up regularly with water if you use them, as they do not hold much water and the level will drop very quickly, especially if you place more than one stem in each cone.)

KITCHENS

The kitchen is often overlooked as a setting for flowers, but country-style kitchens, now common in many city and suburban homes, lend themselves well to rustic floral displays and the use of unconventional containers.

A country kitchen usually exudes a warm, cosy, welcoming atmosphere, suggesting wholesome home cooking and comfort, and the calming image of a self-sufficient, rural lifestyle (that most of us have probably never experienced).

The kitchen is often the hub of the home, where we cook, eat and sometimes entertain; it may even be used more often than the dining or living room. The cook in the household probably spends more waking hours in the kitchen than in any other room in the house. What better reason is there for always having a bowl of flowers or other fresh decoration?

The earthy, natural colours usually used in country kitchen decor look good with decorations in similar colours from the garden. And the materials used can be those associated with cooking and food: vegetables, cut herbs or herbs in pots, seed heads, weeds, fruit and berries.

An additional advantage of having flowers in the kitchen is that they help distract the eye from the clutter of functional utensils and ugly gadgets; but be careful not to allow the flowers to interfere with the main activity of a kitchen.

If you are short of surface space, walls can be used to display wreaths or swags (see the drop on page 54). Country-style wreaths of dried bay leaves, chillies, walnuts, muslin bags of bouquet garni, cinnamon quills and gingham bows look at home in a kitchen. These are also a good idea for the winter months when living materials are expensive or not readily available.

Hanging bunches of dried flowers and herbs is a good way to evoke the feeling of a rambling country garden. To tie them, use natural materials like raffia, hemp or seagrass.

Many traditional kitchen utensils make lovely containers for flower arrangements —

and if they are old and well used or even a bit battered — so much the better.

Herbs as plants also make an attractive and useful decoration in a kitchen (see page 150). An indoor or outdoor window-box full of herbs is a charming idea. Stand the individual planted pots inside the box, so that they can be rotated to give even light and can also be replaced when necessary. Pots of mustard and cress at different growing stages look great, and are edible too.

Plants hanging in front of windows are often in the line of vision and can block some of the natural light. But a line-up on the window-sill can make a kitchen window an attractive focal point.

(see the drop on page 54) ... (see page 150).

ABOVE

A metal fish kettle with a dull, muted surface provides a fitting container for this stylish line-up of vegetables. The pewter plates reinforce the restrained colour theme. The asparagus and small raffia-tied leeks in bunches stand alternately at the back like soldiers. Large florets of cauliflower and whole beetroot with their neatly trimmed stalks are placed in front.
There is no water in this container, but these are vegetables that will remain fairly crisp-looking for a while.

PREVIOUS PAGE

My grandmother's old cast-iron boiler, with many memories of good food, is a lovely holder for this garden-picked mixture of flowers, weeds, herbs and vegetables.
The container is wired (the handle providing a good anchor for the wire) and the flowers are yellow polyanthus, nasturtium, yellow daisies (Euryops pectinatus) and white Marguerites; the wild flowers are buttercups, clover and plantain flowers. The mostly edible greenery, well suited to a kitchen display, includes spinach leaves, bunches of fresh asparagus tied with raffia, rosemary, fennel, angelica leaves and buds, Euphorbia epithymoides and unripe loquat fruit.

RIGHT

The plate rack and dried arrangement set off this unused brick fireplace to advantage. A wooden bird aviary ladder forms a steady base on which to tie or glue an old rolling pin, dried chillies, cinnamon bark, garlic, magnolia leaves, maize, straw, artificial eggs, bay leaves, ginger, pandanas leaf bows, gourds, and tiny clay pots of barley, oats and wheat.

FACING PAGE

The containers for the flowers in this kitchen are two wooden drawers from an old sewing machine table, placed back to back. They have several plastic containers inside them, but are not wired, as the flowers are massed and rest on one another or on the edge of the drawers.
The vibrant red materials include nerine, Alstroemeria, Gomphrena, hawthorn berries, hydrangeas, nandina and the leaves and berries of Virginia creeper (Parthenocissus inserta).

ABOVE

A *very simple, garden-picked mixture of*
heart's-ease (Viola tricolor), *turf lily* (Liriope
muscari) *and lavender, in a blue-spotted*
terracotta jug.

FACING PAGE

Blackberries are a delicious fruit, and
usually free. A simple stoneware jug with a
few stems of wild blackberry, gathered from
the roadside, makes a charming display.

FACING PAGE

Line-ups of flowers look good on this
kitchen mantelpiece, where they can stand
neatly in a row and where the accessories
are also grouped in a formal style. The
terracotta flowerpots have plastic watertight
tumblers inside them.
There is no wire and generous amounts of
multi-coloured zinnias are simply placed in
the water in a posy shape.

ABOVE

This poppy-shaped teapot calls out for
nasturtiums and every year I love arranging
them in it. Use all the nasturtium plant;
flowers, buds, graceful stems, fascinating
leaves and seeds, and let them tumble any
way they choose.

ABOVE

This dainty little pair of marmalade-toned topiaries are just right with this breakfast setting. Their trunks are cinnamon sticks and their fruity tops are artificial oranges, lemons, and crab-apples; tiny wooden apples and pears; starched, orange grosgrain ribbon and reindeer moss. They are shown in the process of being made on page 162.

FACING PAGE

A large antique French baker's stand makes a bold statement in this kitchen; it calls for strong accessories and decorations — don't put little bunches of delicate flowers on a piece like this. A wooden bowl generously piled with ornamental gourds and capsicums, and a rustic bunch of wild fennel seed in a wooden-slatted barrel are in keeping here.

ABOVE

Masses of scarlet zinnias arranged in an
equally bright red enamel flour container
make a warm splash in the corner of this
kitchen. Sprigs of rosemary are the only
added material. The container is wired and
the wire is anchored to the handles at
the top.

FACING PAGE

This kitchen has an exposed brick wall
decorated with a large unit of old spice
drawers. A battered tin farm bucket holds a
dramatic display of lilies (Alocasia odora),
seeds of wild canna (Canna indica) and a
collar of agapanthus leaves: very simple yet
effective. The lilies, by the way, have a
gorgeous perfume.

ABOVE

Growing mustard seed in baby clay pots is a
good idea for a table decoration — one pot
per guest.
The centrepiece at this table is a hollowed-
out squash, filled with floral foam and
water and arranged with fresh garden herbs
including rosemary, dill, tarragon, mint,
and thyme.
The napkins are tied with manila bows and
a sprig of rosemary.

KITCHEN/DINING

Many country-style homes have a dining table in the kitchen, which is a cosy place for eating. If you have the space, or a large bench or refectory table, choose produce from the garden or market for its decorative properties, and compose an edible 'still life'. Heap generous amounts of fruit and vegetables into a trug, large basket or bowl, and set, disguised amongst them, a container of water in which are arranged wild grasses, daisies or interesting vegetable leaves. This is also a good way to make scarce or expensive materials go further. For instance, you may have just a few of the first of the season's daffodils. Put some leaves (their own or others) with them in a jar of water and nestle this into a shallow basket of lemons piled around it, to disguise the jar.

Don't ignore the so-called 'ordinary' vegetables, like potatoes and onions, for they look great massed in a rustic holder, such as a wooden trough. A large bowl or basket of gourds looks right in the kitchen too, but you need to be generous with them, as more impact is achieved this way.

A separate dining room is often used for entertaining, and here you have the opportunity for more formal floral displays. But do not feel that a formal dining room must necessarily have a formal display; a very sophisticated table setting can be decorated with a 'countrified' table centre arrangement, with great success. I have heard this combination described as 'rustic chic' and think the term describes it admirably.

As a general rule flowers on a dining table, where people will be seated to eat, should be at a low enough level for guests to see across them to the other side. And the size of the arrangement should not be too intrusive; people don't want to be fumbling for glasses amongst trails of ivy!

Candles are lovely used in conjunction with flowers. They create a festive mood whether they are used in abundance or in small numbers for an intimate dinner, and candlelight imparts an air of mystery.

When you are arranging a table centre,

remember to echo the shape of the table, with a round arrangement for a round table and an oval or oblong one for a rectangular table.

While you are working on your arrangement, rotate it regularly so that the flowers have a uniform appearance. Don't favour one side with all your best materials and then find that the guests on the other side of the table are staring into gaps or leftovers!

ABOVE

An old white enamel salt-holder that has had the lid removed has been wired and holds a simple bunch of asters, roses, Japanese anemones, Lavandula spica 'Alba', hydrangeas and touches of grey foliage. The arrangement makes a pleasing contrast against a collection of blue and white china on a kitchen dresser.

ABOVE

Mixed pink cottage-garden flowers glow in a
round wired tin bowl. They bring a warm
touch to a country living room decorated in
natural colours.

The flowers include asters 'Harringtons
Pink', Michaelmas daisies, balloon flowers
(Platycodon), *Japanese anemones 'Prince
Henry',* Phlox paniculata, *verbena,*
hydrangeas, Rehmannia elata, *and mixed
grey foliages.*

BEDROOMS

Flowers in a bedroom should be kept simple, unless you have lots of space.

I favour jugs of simple garden mixtures or specimen vases of one or two garden-picked roses. Soft colours are usually more soothing, too, unless you want to enhance existing strong colour as I have done with the deep pink flowers against the quilts on page 71.

RIGHT

A child's bedroom calls for a simple flower arrangement. This enamel kitchen jug holds asters, roses, Platycodon, Japanese anemones, and dianthus.

FACING PAGE

FACING PAGE

An inviting corner of this guest bedroom shows an alcove above the bed holding a blonde willow trug, which has a wired metal liner.
The flower mix includes Boltonia, *Marguerite daisies which are all forms of* Chrysanthemum frutescens, euphorbia, *and wild grasses.*

RIGHT

A sunny touch in a bedroom corner. A bright yellow-painted basket has a wired plastic bowl liner set inside it with a rim-level ring of pale coloured moss. Yellow and white irises have all been cut the same length and massed in the centre.
An off-white paper tie bridges the gap.

ABOVE

*The paint finish in this bedroom makes a
pretty backdrop for this arrangement.
A ragged moss basket holds a wired plastic
bowl and is mounded with miniature pink
roses and the lovely green rose
Rosa chinensis 'Viridiflora'.*

FACING PAGE

*A collection of old quilts stored in a
bedroom make a multi-coloured background
for a lavish pink arrangement.
The container is a wired shallow pewter
bowl. The flowers are asters, phlox, achillea
and cornflowers and the pink-tinted leaves
are sage, Irisene and berberis.*

BATHROOMS

Flowers might be considered an unusual accessory for a bathroom, but if the decor is clinical, flowers will bring warmth to the room.

Country-style bathrooms are likely to have a homely decor, with perhaps a clutter of interesting collectables, which lend themselves to a mixed garden bunch.

As surface space is often at a premium, I suggest jugs or other upright containers that only use air space. Keep the display simple and small.

The humid atmosphere of a bathroom can also be a good place for certain pot plants, provided the light source is adequate.

RIGHT

A terracotta jug filled with a casual mixture of sunny yellow flowers suits a natural wood country bathroom.

FACING PAGE

The blue of the old tiles and handbasin is echoed in a jug of mixed blue and white flowers.

CHAPTER THREE

SPECIAL OCCASIONS

CELEBRATIONS OFFER THE OPPORtunity to decorate in a special way. It may be a grand affair or a small family gathering. The celebration may have a theme, or a particular colour scheme or it may incorporate some appropriate accessories. Whatever the occasion, you can create a festive atmosphere with flowers.

FACING PAGE

Grandma's birthday — a time to bring out this collection of old floral-patterned china for a birthday tea. The large jug is filled with a selection of mixed blue and purple flowers: Lisianthus, cornflowers, delphiniums, gentian, and eryngium. The plain Madeira cake has a wreath of complementary flowers including delphiniums, cornflowers, verbena, heliotrope (for devotion) and rosemary. Rosemary is also tucked into the blue bow of the birthday gift.

This is one time when you can be adventurous and possibly change the whole look of a room with decorations. If you are working with a large space, remember to place arrangements where they will catch the eye, but not obscure important things. A few arrangements on a grand scale will have more impact in a large area than many small arrangements dotted about. Remember, too, that flowers are often seen only from a distance.

Sometimes space is scarce, but in this case flowers can be made into decorations to be hung high on walls, on light fittings, over doorways or attached to poles and pillars.

Take care to place your arrangements where they will have maximum impact and not be easily knocked over.

Think of the occasion as a whole. Meticulous planning will help to make the end result a success, and make your task more enjoyable.

ST. VALENTINE'S DAY

St. Valentine's Day, on 14 February, is the traditional day when love tokens are exchanged, sometimes anonymously. A popular token is a gift of flowers.

The giving of red roses is a custom believed to have been originated by Louis XVI of France, who sent them to his wife, Marie Antoinette.

The bright red tussie mussie, on page 119, was inspired by the verse about tomatoes, (the 'love-apple') and the lovely little round handkerchief that my mother gave me as a child.

A meal for two can be given a romantic look by using a heart shape in table linen, candles, or china or in a shape created with flowers. Even food can be prepared in a heart shape — heart-shaped cake tins are available or you could make heart-shaped pastries (palmiers) such as those in the photo on the facing page.

RIGHT

Naturally I have used a heart shape as the base for this Valentine's wreath of vines. The raffia-tied terracotta hearts reinforce the shape. Ivy (for friendship, fidelity and marriage) is twined around the heart, bunches of roses (for love), and jasmine (for amiability) are tied at the top with dark green ribbon, which also forms the tie by which the wreath hangs.

FACING PAGE

A romantic setting for two. Freesias, roses, dianthus, jasmine and other pretty garden items make up a simple table centre arrangement for a Valentine's meal. Soft candlelight is dispersed by placing heating candles, in china heart shapes, in moss. The gift is accompanied by a wooden painted Shaker hand with a romantic message and a posy of tiny red roses.

EASTER

Easter is the time when we remember Christ's crucifixion and resurrection, and when the beginning of spring is celebrated in the Northern Hemisphere. Eggs have been a symbol of the renewal of life for centuries, and they can be successfully incorporated into floral decorations suitable for this festival.

Special breads, hot cross buns, simnel cake and, of course, eggs are all enjoyed at Easter and a table decoration can be made to complement these foods.

You might like to try making nests out of straw or moss. Fill them with tiny, realistic candy eggs to give as gifts. Wrapped in cellophane and tied with a piece of string, they look irresistible. Or make home-made fondant eggs and colour them. Candied primroses would also be a lovely addition, or you could try making your own chocolate eggs.

RIGHT

An Easter table setting. A yellow-painted, polythene-lined basket containing floral foam is sprinkled with straw (to give the impression of a nest) and filled with mostly yellow flowers and pussy willow. Blown hen's eggs are scattered over the straw amongst the flowers. Quail's eggs and tiny, speckled, egg-like candles nestle in the hand-made birds' nests in the front. The large egg candles have the tops cut off to reveal the yolk-coloured wax.

FACING PAGE

Some simple ideas for Easter table accessories. A single yellow polyanthus plant is potted into an old clay pot and tied with a generous, bright yellow and white gingham ribbon. Little clay pots, edged with moss and tied with rich gold velvet ribbons, also make good holders for candles. The eggs are quail's eggs, available from most delicatessen shops.

Children respond to bright, primary colours.
This cheerful table setting sits on a wreath of
floral foam, with a sphere in the centre.
Bright lollipops are spiked into the centre
ball, together with some of the flowers. The
remainder of the anemones and spray
chrysanthemums are anchored into the
wreath. Angelica adds a touch of shiny,
dark green.

FACING PAGE

A novel idea for a display at an afternoon tea
for a sewing group. An old sewing box has
several plastic containers placed inside it and
is massed with cornflowers, dianthus, roses,
lavender, heliotrope, spray chrysanthemums
and mixed grey foliages. The collection of old
embroidery pieces completes the scene.

HOGMANAY

A formal dinner for a Scottish family and friends celebrating Hogmanay (New Year's Eve).

RIGHT

The door decoration welcomes friends to the house. It has a large base of preserved conifer (which means it will keep indefinitely). The central decoration comprises cones, larch, a preserved holly-like foliage, lichen, and the thistle-like tops of Echinops and Eryngium. Tartan fabric (not ribbon) was used to make the bow and the table-napkins continue the theme at the meal table.

FACING PAGE

The tartan table-napkins were the inspiration for colours in this table centre arrangement — lots of green and just a touch of red and purple. The contents include angelica, conifer, euphorbia, holly, ivy, Echinops, Eryngium, chive flowers, fresh cherries and a green candle.

This mantelpiece in a formal dining room has been transformed into a countryside scene featuring a stuffed pheasant set amongst bulrushes, copper beech, oats and many other dried components.
The whole of the tableau has been arranged piece by piece using blocks of dry floral foam securely glued on to a card the length of the mantel. The base is disguised by straw, moss and lichen and the upright pieces gracefully frame the mirror above the mantel, creating an attractive outside edge.

RIGHT

A hearty lunch in a holiday house. The theme of fishing and shooting is reinforced with the use of an old fishing creel, which has been painted dark green. It has a wired plastic bowl of water inside it and is arranged with the rich greens of Magnolia grandiflora, Michelia figo, and berries of privet and Callicarpa. The black seeds are Aristea ecklonii.

WEDDINGS

Flowers help set the scene for a wedding, and bouquets, headdresses, church, reception and home decorations are an important part of the occasion.

It is necessary to plan the flowers as far ahead as possible, making sure that they are suited to the style of the wedding, and the colour of the dresses.

Flowers traditionally used for weddings, such as roses and stephanotis, can be given a country look by adding garden snippets like ivy, variegated or scented geranium leaves, lavender, and even delicate berries and seeds.

RIGHT

A posy to go with a dress of oyster-coloured polka dot linen damask. The flowers are 'Pamela' roses, the pale pink form of Nerine bowdenii, *and peachy pink bouvardia. The wide, oyster-coloured velvet ribbon adds another texture.*

FACING PAGE

A lavender hedge is the backdrop for this cool, alfresco lunch setting. The subtle colours in the plaid table mats inspired this choice of flowers, vegetables and foliage. I first lined an old wire basket with moss, and then put in a wire-filled plastic bowl to hold the arrangement. The mixture includes aubergine-coloured tulips, cherry pie (Heliotropium arborescens), *campanula, borage flowers,* Brunnera macrophylla, Cerinthe retorta, *globe artichokes, and the leaves of bronze fennel, rosemary, conifer, variegated ivy and* Lychnis coronaria alba.

The flower-girl's smart Black Watch tartan skirt was my starting point for planning the flowers for this wedding. Strong dark green, blue and black colours are not usually associated with weddings, and they offered a challenge.

In consultation with the bride-to-be and her mother, I decided on a fresh flower pomander for the flower-girl. A ball of flowers is an easy way for children to carry flowers — they do not have to worry about the way it should be held for it can be viewed from any angle. Make sure the cord of the pomander is not too long for a child.

The flowers used in this pomander matched the 'Porcelina' roses, lavender and a mixture of dainty white flowers in the bride's and the adult bridesmaids' bouquets. I popped in loops of Black Watch tartan ribbon and used a sophisticated black cord and tassel.

FACING PAGE

The reception table setting reflects the smart look of the tartan. Old, weathered clay flowerpots in three sizes hold chunky green candles and are arranged with a mixture of the same flowers, mostly roses and mixed foliage, including graceful ivy trails. As well as the Black Watch ribbon, I introduced some plain ribbons in the exact colours of the tartan, and the table-cloth, napkins, china and place-name cards all reinforce the theme.

LEFT

This romantic three-tiered wedding cake has very elaborate, lacy frills on each tier and the icing has the slightest apricot blush of colour, which enhances the decorative 'Porcelina' roses. Queen Anne's lace is the only other flower, except for the white Nigella scattered amongst the tulle swathing the base.

LEFT AND ABOVE

The bride wore ivory silk and carried a wired bouquet of 'Porcelina' roses with their own foliage, Queen Anne's lace and a touch of variegated ivy. Hidden at the back of the bouquet was a collection of tiny snippets of good luck symbols: rosemary for remembrance, marjoram for blushes, white rose to say 'I am worthy of you', parsley for festivity, thyme for activity, sage for domestic virtue, white jasmine for amiability, violet for faithfulness, mint for virtue and heart's-ease to say 'You occupy my thoughts'. There was also a tiny blue flower and a blue ribbon to represent the old adage, 'Something old, something new, something borrowed, something blue'.

LEFT

The adult bridesmaids silk as the bride and ca posies of roses, narcissu touch of lavender a including acid-gr

FACING PAGE

A romantic wired hair circlet for a bride. The white flowers, some of which have a beautiful perfume, are stephanotis, jasmine, Nerine bowdenii 'Alba', Rosa chinensis 'Viridiflora', and lime-green clusters of Backhousia citriodora. The back of the circlet is finished with a full-blown garden rose, 'Grüss-an-Aachen', and two buds.

The decorations in this candlescape include trails of ivy woven around the elegant, French-style hanging candelabra.

The terracotta pot has a wreath sitting neatly at the rim with a generous bunch of miniature apricot roses arranged around the candle.

The large vine wreath on the table has four corrugated caramel candles sitting inside it. Strewn around the bases of the candles are hydrangea heads, and nandina berries, which don't require water. Dried camellias are glued at intervals around the wreath.

A pair of tall iron candlesticks have plastic 'candle-cups' secured on to the tops. A fat green candle and wet floral foam, into which fresh flowers, berries and trails of bare birch twigs are set, sits in each one.

The candelabra on the right has a platform which holds three bowls of wet floral foam from which a mass of flowers and foliage descend.

The remainder of the decorated candles have flowers, leaves and berries around their bases.

HARVEST FESTIVAL
Most religions celebrate the gathering of the harvest each year. In North America, the custom of Thanksgiving commemorates the bringing-in of the first successful harvest planted by 17th-century settlers.

Churches all over the world are decorated with grains, particularly wheat and barley, vegetables, fruit, flowers and home-made produce during the harvest festival.

This setting creates a scene of plenty: giant golden sunflowers casually arranged in an old copper watering can and a dried wreath made of miniature strawberry maize, together with walnuts, potatoes, gourds and spring onions, and an old painted wheelbarrow laden with vegetables.

HALLOWE'EN

This is the time when the souls of the dead wander the earth. In Britain the turnip is used to make Hallowe'en lanterns, but in America the turnip has been replaced by the pumpkin.

Pumpkins and gourds have been the inspiration for this setting, and here they are as part of a wreath, or waiting to be made into lanterns or decorate a table setting. The tiny gourds in the pots would look good with a candle placed in each hollowed-out top.

CHRISTMAS

This is a time for traditional country themes, and I enjoy using lots of greenery, red and white flowers, and fruit. Natural cones and nuts are useful, too, and I like to mix them in with branches, moss and conifer. I very rarely colour the cones, and if man-made items are called for, I look for artificial berries and suchlike in colours that are as natural as possible. I search for commercially made decorations in subtle, natural colours, like the pewter bells on page 104 or the terracotta shapes on page 106, and prefer to use all of one colour and not to mix them up. However, of course there are situations where bright colours are called for.

Evergreen foliages symbolising perpetual life have long been used in festive decoration. The Norsemen and the Romans used them, and they were also part of early pagan rituals. Greenery associated with Christmas includes laurel, bay, holly, ivy, yew, mistletoe and conifers. The red berries of holly are thought by some to represent drops of Christ's blood, and the sharp spines on the leaves, His crown of thorns. Evergreens became fashionable symbols on Victorian Christmas cards, as a promise that 'our friendship will be evergreen'.

The Christmas tree was introduced in England by Queen Victoria's husband, Prince Albert, in 1841. Hessian troops in the English Army took the idea of a tree to America during the War of Independence.

LEFT

This beautiful staircase hardly needs decorating, but at Christmas it's irresistible. The garland has an artificial base, with wired sprays of artificial conifer that are perfect for holding the fresh pieces entwined into it. Evergreens that last out of water are ivy, conifer, bay and holly. The large hanging cluster at the foot of the stairs is arranged in a suspended 'cage' of wet floral foam. This is attached to the newel post with wire at the top and bottom, disguised by ivy, and it makes a bold punctuation mark with which to complete the garland. The red capsicums add traditional Christmas colour.

The use of candles and lights probably came from Martin Luther, who, in the early 16th century, used a candlelit tree to represent the starry heaven from which Christ came.

The Christmas Rose *Helleborus niger*, is associated with Christmas in the Northern Hemisphere as it flowers through the winter.

The use of the scarlet poinsettia has come to us from North America. The plant originates from Mexico, where it was known as the Flower of the Holy Night.

Wreaths were introduced to America by Scandinavian immigrants and more recently, they have gained popularity in Britain. They are a versatile and attractive way of making a Christmas decoration. They can be hung on a wall or door; suspended from a ceiling so they hang horizontally, face down; or placed on a table.

LEFT

A conical shape made of tree roots provides an intriguing alternative to the traditional Christmas tree. It is a base that you could keep, and ring the changes each year. (It could also be used to train ivy to grow on as a topiary shape.) Fresh chestnuts, given a little extra gleam with furniture polish, have been glued on to the frame. Sprigs of fresh conifer, holly, and clusters of chillies provide the green; and red capsicums tied with red grosgrain ribbon add a festive touch. The sprigs of greenery will need to be replaced over the Christmas period.

ABOVE

A commercially available cone tree is decorated simply by glueing dried capsicums, clusters of mixed nuts, and raffia-tied bunches of cinnamon quills to the branches. The fragile, fresh apricots have been gently wired and attached; they will have a short life, but add a magic, glowing blush to this unusual tree.

FACING PAGE

The beautiful French Christmas plates here were my inspiration for this cake wreath. The plates are decorated with holly leaves and berries of an unusual burnt orange colour instead of the traditional bright holly red.

The rich fruit cake, sitting on a natural wooden platter, has a caramelised topping of dried fruit and nuts, without the usual glacé cherries, to keep the colours to brown and orange.

The evergreens include ivy, box, rosemary, bay, conifer, and holly that has had its red berries replaced by artificial orange ones, to match the plates, as does the blue ribbon, perhaps a surprising touch in a Christmas mixture.

An antique Russian sledge makes an
appropriate base for this fresh Christmas
arrangement. A shallow tray of floral foam
sits on the top of the sledge, secured with
adhesive. The flowers are red anemones and
perfumed, white lilies (Lilium longiflorum
hybrid), while the Christmas evergreens
include ivy, bay, holly, larch, and
other conifers.

ABOVE

The plastic green and cream berries in this
arrangement look authentic nestled
into fresh foliage.
I have used the traditional Christmas foliages
of holly and ivy, but the variegated varieties
tone well with the colour theme.
The floral components are Helleborus niger,
Lisianthus flowers and their beautiful buds,
and camellias; the foliage includes conifers,
variegated ivy and Osmanthus
heterophyllus 'Varigatus' (false holly).
A touch of cream reindeer moss adds
another texture.

LEFT

The natural colours of grey, green and brown
go beautifully with this pale stone fireplace
surmounted by a collection of English
majolica plates.
Wooden aviary ladders, painted dark green,
form a stable foundation to which objects
have been tied, wired or glued. The materials
include lichen-covered branches, preserved
conifer, cones, moss, huge sticks of cinnamon
bark and pewter bells, the only
man-made item.
The cone topiaries placed in a formal line on
the mantelpiece stand in clay pots, packed
with green reindeer moss, and the grey ribbon
used on the duller undersides adds a subtle
trimming. The candles are set in old
tin patty pans.

FACING PAGE

This dramatic line-up of cone topiaries looks
wonderful at Christmas and beyond as they
last indefinitely and require no care.
See the descriptions on pages 162 and 163 for
instructions on how to make them. The
containers are miniature wooden Versailles
tubs, lined with moss, and the cones are
Douglas fir, Monterey cypress,
larch and pine.

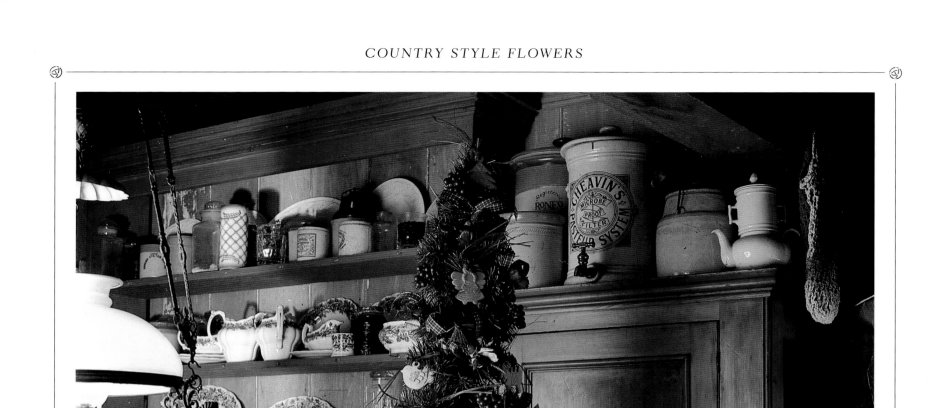

FACING PAGE

Some artificial trees are most attractive and make very good substitutes for the real thing. This one has terracotta tree decorations in several different motifs: bells, angels, trees, birds and goats. They are tied with burgundy-coloured raffia, which complements the colour of the bunches of artificial berries and dried roses. Each bunch of roses is tied with a toning bow of ribbon.

LEFT

This huge wreath has a base of vine peeping attractively through the branches of conifer and bare larch. Fresh ivy leaves and cones add bolder detail. The tie is a huge hank of bleached jute. The greens, greys and browns are earthy and restful, and give the wreath a country, Christmassy look. See the instructions for assembling a wreath on page 163. The conifers are Cedrus deodara (Indian cedar) and Cupressus glabra.

Wired bunches of fresh cherries bring this rustic wreath alive. Trails of fresh ivy are entwined amongst the vine and a double bow of bottle green and rich, red ribbon make up the trimming.

FACING PAGE

A Southern Hemisphere Christmas lunch — alfresco. Christmas in summertime means no red holly berries, hellebores, or other winter flowers. Evergreens, of course, are still available and this table centre arrangement employs holly, bay, box, ivy and the lovely greyish green cedar, Cedrus atlantica 'Glauca', *with red capsicums to add the traditional Christmas colour. The napkin rings are made from wired snippets of cedar.*

CHAPTER FOUR

FLOWERS AS GIFTS

*Detail of a box trimmed with a wired spray
of preserved oak leaves and dried cups with
their acorns glued into them.*

SPECIAL OCCASIONS ARE ALSO celebrated by the giving of gifts, and flowers are probably one of the oldest, most traditional and acceptable of presents. A country-style posy of flowers and garden bits and pieces chosen and prepared by a friend are much more expressive than a bought bouquet.

FACING PAGE

Ordinary brown paper, corrugated cardboard, bark cloth and recycled paper are part of this display of wrapping ideas along with hand-marbled paper, tissue paper and bought paper bags. The packing includes cigarette paper and wood straw, and the ties are jute, hemp, linen thread, twisted seagrass, raffia, pandanas leaf, and man-made ribbons and ties in natural colours.
Look for extra ideas in handcraft supply shops and haberdashers, as well as stationers.

The symbolic language of flowers can make the gift even more special. The Austrians have a charming tradition in the Gewürzsträussl (which I have adapted on page 115). This is an everlasting posy that originated in Salzburg and dates from the beginning of the 19th century. It consists of herbs and spices, to symbolise good luck and fertility and they traditionally use preserved *Ruscus* for foliage. It can be a special present for a bride on her wedding day, but it is also popular throughout Austria as a good luck souvenir.

The ancient tussie mussie, although it probably had a medicinal origin (for it was composed mostly of herbs), conveys a special meaning too, usually romantic — a lovely way to communicate one's sentiments to someone special.

Of course, a posy doesn't have to have a message; it could just be a spontaneously gathered bunch of garden treasures. Or you

may choose to arrange garden or bought flowers in a pretty basket with a bow trimming, which the recipient can then just put in a chosen space without needing to think about arranging the flowers.

A bouquet or arrangement of dried flowers is also a most acceptable alternative.

LEFT

An array of beautifully presented gifts provides ideas for wrapping items of many shapes and sizes.
Dried hydrangeas tone perfectly with grape-coloured tissue.
A dried camellia with an ikat fabric tie trims another grape-coloured box.
Dried chillies look stunning alongside a canary-yellow cotton upholstery tape bow on checked paper.
Christmas pot-pourri looks inviting in a cylinder-shaped box covered with hand-marbled paper.
Fresh green bay leaves decorate a box wrapped with soft bark and tied with bleached jute.
A single, dried, pink peony, with its buds and leaves, enhances rich peony-patterned paper. The straw net ribbon gives the package a country look.
A veined, preserved leaf tied with rust-coloured raffia threaded through the card lies on brown wrapping.
A large, skeletonised magnolia leaf decorates a brown tissue-wrapped box, which has a finely folded line of natural tissue incorporated in the self-coloured tie.
Fresh viburnum berries trim fruit-patterned French paper tied with a tomato-red grosgrain ribbon.
Wooden clothes pegs seal rose hips and a dried camellia with matching cards on to interestingly patterned paper bags.
The long box on the left is a lidded wooden box used originally for a bottle of wine, but recycled to hold clay flowerpots resting on cigarette paper.

Herbs and kitchen-garden plants make a useful, often aromatic, and attractive present, especially if they are placed in interesting holders.

The rustic metal basket in this photograph holds six varieties of thyme: lemon variegated thyme, silver thyme, common thyme, woolly thyme, golden thyme and spreading emerald carpet thyme.

The battered old wooden tool box holds three varieties of basil — sweet basil, spicy globe basil and purple basil.

The tarragon plant would be a thoughtful choice for a cook.

Sage was the inspiration for an imaginative gift of an old, well-used metal colander, fresh onions and an attractively hand-written recipe for sage and onion stuffing.

The chives are planted in an antique copper trough, which makes an acceptable present in itself. The artichokes would be for someone with a little more garden space than the herb plants need.

The terracotta name plates add a decorative but practical touch.

RIGHT

Here I have adapted a traditional Austrian posy, using box leaves, which will eventually dry out to a parchment colour.

The spices I have used in the bouquet are cloves, nutmeg, cinnamon bark, vanilla, ginger, almond kernel, nutmeg, pepper, star anise, juniper, laurel and pimento, and the posy makes an intriguing little gift. It does, however, require wiring, like a bridal bouquet. The text for the greeting card to go with it reads:

This is an aromatic bouquet, combining many different spices for perfume, flavour and taste. It brings a special wish: May all ill be turned away from your door, and wherever you go may you find health, happiness and God's special blessing and protection.

ABOVE

The large country bunch of flowers in this attractive trug includes amber and gold and rust-coloured spray chrysanthemums, Boltonia, euphorbia and fennel seeds. Brown eggs, honey in the comb and warm, freshly baked bread complete the gift.

FACING PAGE

The frill on the red posy is a circular handkerchief patterned with tomatoes, oranges, lemons and limes — an additional gift in itself.
The stems of the posy had to be cut quite short to fit inside the handkerchief and allow for a generous frill. The handkerchief was starched to stand out, and, of course, would be removed when the recipient puts the posy in water.
The red flowers and foliage include roses for love, rosemary for remembrance, strawberry blossom for foresight, box leaves for stoicism and angelica for inspiration. The other flowers and leaves are pineapple sage, Gomphrena, bouvardia, geraniums, and nandina, and the berries are Viburnum opulus 'Americanum' and a lone alpine strawberry. The basket of tiny, pear-shaped tomatoes reinforces the theme.

The yellow tussie mussie is surrounded by a doyley and holds roses, solidaster freesias, French marigolds, and wallflowers; the greenery includes scented geranium leaves, Stachys byzantina, parsley seed, Euphorbia robbiae and variegated ivy.
White flowers make up the third posy enclosed in a white paper doyley, with a base of green hydrangeas and roses, cornflowers, freesias, jasmine, Osteospermun, variegated apple mint, peppermint geranium and tiny dianthus.

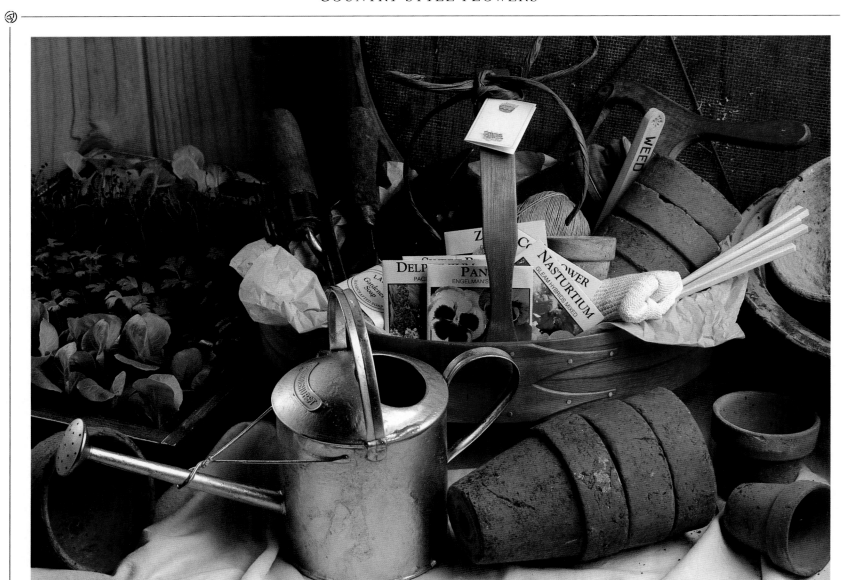

ABOVE

*A fine, new Shaker basket is heaped with
cottage-garden seeds, old hand tools, baby
flowerpots, cotton-knit gardening gloves, a
cake of gardener's soap and an apron.
The blue-painted wooden tray is full of
salad seedlings: Tom Thumb and Green
Thumb lettuces, Red Steak spring onions
and Utah celery.*

Plants, especially if you re-pot them into a specially chosen container, are another idea; or, for the gardener, a selection of bulbs, along with some potting mix and a bulb bowl or flowerpot.

Another gardener's gift idea is a basket (like the Shaker basket pictured on facing page), which is a gift in itself, filled with seeds, tools, gardening gloves, and perhaps a gardening book — there are many possibilities here.

Presents of food accompanied by flowers, always look attractive. Home-made preserves or other kitchen produce, or fresh fruit and vegetables, can be attractively presented in a country basket with a small posy or generous garden bunch of flowers added. Commercially bought produce could be given a homespun look in this way, too.

Or the gift may be the container itself, like a beautiful antique basket, an interesting old kitchen container or the old printer's tray on this page; filling it with something appropriate adds another dimension — food for thought.

Once you have begun to explore all the possibilities of making gifts out of natural materials, you will find many exciting combinations are possible.

LEFT

An unusual idea for a container is an antique printer's tray laden with spices. From left to right: cloves, coriander, cardamom, allspice, fenugreek, pickling spices, lemon grass, mace, juniper berries, star anise, nutmegs, black peppercorns, chillies, cinnamon sticks, bay leaves and dried ginger. Vanilla pods are tied with a natural-coloured coarse cotton bow, and an old nutmeg grater adds a practical finishing touch.

FACING PAGE

*A simple gift that conveys a breath of spring.
A single yellow polyanthus plant is placed,
still in its pot, in a polythene-lined, mossy
basket. Bare tortured-willow twigs have been
twisted around the handle to give the basket
an added ragged look. Fresh moss is packed
around the plant to disguise the pot and
plastic liner, and to give it the look of a lush
forest floor. The moss will die but some
varieties will still hold their attractive colour
and texture for a long time.*

LEFT

*A sunny bouquet. Choose all-yellow flowers,
which could be either bought or garden
grown, or a combination of both. This
bouquet includes freesias, antirrhinum,
solidasters, miniature roses, sprigs of rosemary
and variegated ivy from the garden.
The flowers have been arranged in the hand,
with the stems being placed at angles one by
one. The stems are not tied until the bouquet
is complete, but an alternative method would
be to tie the stems as you proceed.
Doubled-over, striped yellow and white tissue
provides the frill at the base, and two sheets
of plain, bright yellow tissue back the
bouquet and enclose the stems. A generous
yellow gingham ribbon covers the end of the
tissue and completes the picture.*

The pastel-coloured flowers are massed tightly together to give an abundant effect, and include roses, French lavender, scabious and cornflowers in several colours, palest pink spray chrysanthemums, micro-dianthus, blue Didiscus caeruleus, tweedia and mauve Michaelmas daisies. The ribbon complements the tones of the flowers.

This moss basket is lined with a plastic bowl to hold floral foam. Long ivy trails are spiked into the floral foam to keep them fresh, and they are then entwined around the rim and handles of the basket. They are neatly wired where necessary, but the basket is so raggedy this is not needed in many places.

FACING PAGE

A lovely idea for a Christmas present. Fresh ivy trims the edge of this Spanish basket, which has holly-patterned ceramic handles. All the contents have been chosen in natural colours to complement the scented candle. The basket is lined with preserved leaves and wood straw and is generously filled with huge walnuts, pistachios, hazelnuts, macadamias, home-made tissue-wrapped chocolates and cellophane-wrapped toffees. Jute-tied cigars and an old nutcracker add a personal touch.

LEFT

A bouquet of dried lavender, delphinium and gentian, wrapped in two shades of blue tissue paper and tied with a length of woven cotton.

RIGHT

This rich berry basket is accompanied by a small garden posy in complementary colours. The tiny antique trug is lined with peppermint geranium leaves and blueberries, raspberries and cultivated blackberries. The tissue-wrapped posy holds china roses, antirrhinum 'Red Rocket', dianthus 'Barbara', fuchsia berries, berberis, campanula 'Blue Chips', Lantana montevidensis, spiraea, lacecap hydrangea 'Greyswood', verbena 'Mauve Queen', and purple-leafed sage.

CHAPTER FIVE

DRIED FLOWERS

*The base of a Chinese steamer basket
makes an interesting container for this
natural-coloured arrangement. The dried
flowers are matricaria.*

DRIED FLOWERS ADD ANOTHER
dimension to the range of options open to
flower-arrangers. They last, a very positive
advantage these days, so they are good value
compared to buying fresh flowers every week.

Dried flowers are often no more expensive
than their fresh counterparts, and some of
them have such subtle, soft, faded tones.
Their textures can be lovely, too. They require
less care — no watering and tending — and
they can be used in ways in which you
couldn't use fresh flowers, such as in hanging
bunches or sculpted topiaries.

*A selection of dried flowers, seeds and
foliage, They include yellow achillea, orange
safflower, roses, larkspur, lavender,
amaranthus, Echinops, acanthus, matricaria,
delphinium, Nigella seeds, ixodia, and barley.*

You may wish to grow flowers especially for
drying. Some that are easy to grow include
larkspur, statice, achillea, lavender, *Nigella* and
helichrysum. Or buy fresh flowers (if you
don't have a garden) especially to dry, or buy
some choice dried specimens and supplement
them with inexpensive, home-dried varieties.
Remember, too, that many weeds have lovely
seeds to dry, such as dock or wild carrot (see
the group on page 136). It's also worth know-
ing that bulrushes will last longer if sprayed
with hairspray immediately after picking.

It is important to pick or buy plant materials
for drying at the correct stage of ripeness;
earlier rather than later is a good rule. Roses
are better in bud, as once they have opened
or are full-blown, they will drop. Be prepared
for dramatic colour changes in some roses
when they dry. If grasses are picked too ripe
they will shatter on drying — in fact most
things that have begun to set seed will disinte-

grate on drying. Hydrangeas are an exception, as they should be picked for drying at a late stage, when their colours have become more muted and their petals slightly leathery.

There are basically three methods of preserving flowers: naturally, in the air; in a desiccant; and in glycerine.

The hanging method is the simplest. I use clothes-drying racks, but any kind of structure that has one or several crossbars is suitable. Flowers look lovely in the process of drying, so you may wish to choose a visible place, although the darker, drier and more airy it is, the better. The ideal environment is in an area where the air is dry, warm and moving and is also as dark as possible; requirements which are not always available in a home environment.

When you are preparing flowers for hanging, gather them in small bunches, and leave gaps between them on the drying rack. Making thick bunches and hanging them too close together could prevent the air from circulating between them and cause mildew. I use rubber bands to secure the stems, because they contract as the stems shrink when the moisture evaporates, and continue to hold the stems in place. String holds stems adequately when they are fresh, but once they begin to dry, they tend to fall out.

RIGHT

Roses, lavender, safflower and barley are drying on an old wooden clothes rack. Baby terracotta pots of dried roses, and a wooden barrel, also filled with roses, stand at its base.

FACING PAGE

A huge, dried arrangement set on a low table against a Victorian scrap-screen. The rustic wooden pail, with a rope handle, holds a rich tapestry of dried roses, larkspur, safflower, achillea, delphinium, lavender and sea holly (Eryngium), *and the pail edge is trimmed with a generous swathe of pale green lichen. The stems are placed in wire mesh netting in exactly the same way as a fresh arrangement would be.*

I tend to break the rules when arranging dried flowers, and yet they still work. I like doing straight-sided, upright styles, many of them with flat tops. I prefer not to mix colours up too much; I like subtle, tone-on-tone mixtures. But there are exceptions, like the huge mixture on page 131, which enhances the rich colours in the busy scrap-screen.

I think it's important to be generous with your ingredients. An abundant look has much more impact than a wispy, sparse arrangement that looks as though you couldn't afford quite enough flowers. If you haven't got many flowers, use a smaller container.

Many dried flowers are small, and they will look better either massed together in one container or in clumps of one type — not dotted about singly.

I do sometimes use artificial materials, such as berries or ribbon, when I want to introduce a colour and/or texture that dried plants do not provide — or just for a surprise element. That is why I needed the touch of blue paper in the topiaries on page 134, and the bright artificial berries in the marmalade-toned topiaries on page 60.

Another exception is the preserved foliage, which has had dye put into the preservative; but the colours are true to life, like the realistic copper beech on page 138. I buy these leaves prepared in this way.

You may prefer not to use dried flowers at all — and certainly, even in the winter months, there is always greenery or a bowl of bright oranges or attractive vegetables. But many people find dried materials very satisfying to work with for they have a distinctive character all their own.

ABOVE

An upright, black basket arranged with dried, dark red roses against a background of French toile de Jouy and plates.

FACING PAGE

A mixture of wheat, oats, barley and quaking grass in a biodegradable planter. The restful colours are particularly suitable for the corner of this room.

FACING PAGE

A stately pair of huge dried topiaries. Large Spanish terracotta urns with an antique finish are the elegant holders for this formal country pair.

The materials used are reindeer moss in cream and pale green, sprigs of blue sea holly (Eryngium), and snippets of blue paper ribbon.

The cones include Douglas fir, banksia, pine and eucalyptus gum nuts with a lovely grey blush. Don't be tempted to paint or colour the cones; the charm of this combination is subtle, natural colour.

A generous amount of moss is heaped around the base, to disguise the plaster and plastic buckets.

The blue wool plaid throw and the yellow antique porcelain melons add to this striking grouping.

Further instructions for assembling these and other dried topiaries are on pages 162-3.

LEFT

A large, bleached cane basket arranged for a fireplace gives a contrast of yellow and blue with a touch of cream. Larkspur, delphinium, lavender, and gentian provide the blue colour, and the rich, mustard colour comes from achillea and roses. Larkspur also gives the cream shade.

The basket can be lined with plastic or paper, with floral foam as the base. The foam can be made to stand up slightly above the level of the basket so that some stems can fall gracefully over the basket's sides. Cover it at the completion of the arrangement with flowers (achillea in this case) and foliage (rose leaves) placed deep in the basket.

RIGHT

RIGHT

A rough-hewn wooden barrel with metal
banding makes a great container for this
mixture of roadside weeds which have been
dried and set on a stencilled bathroom floor.
The weeds include dock seeds, timothy grass
and fescue and pandanas leaf forms the tie
and bow. Because the stems are so massed in
this container, they support each other, and
no wire or other support is needed.

FACING PAGE

An old wooden tea box sits amongst this
collection of kitchen objects. These soft
neutral colours and the texture of wood
complement rather than detract from the
arrangement. The dried materials in the box
are matricaria (at the top), amaranthus
(centre) and ixodia daisy (bottom). A thick
hank of bleached jute is twisted and tied
around the base. The arrangement has a
base of floral foam and the stems are placed
in compact rows.

RIGHT

An autumnal mixture of preserved foliages, which are everlasting. This copper casserole dish looks good with bronze colours. The leaves are magnolia, oak, eucalyptus (silver dollar gum), and copper beech.

FACING PAGE

A dried topiary made in accordance with the instructions given on page 163, but on a smaller scale. The materials used are black reindeer moss, achillea, safflower, Chinese lantern, larch cones, walnuts, rust-coloured artificial berries and green paper and straw-like ribbon. The topiary stands in a weathered terracotta pot, looking at home amongst these green, terracotta and yellow accessories.

ABOVE

A mass of lavender suitable for a bedroom setting, in a green-painted wire basket and lined with sage-green moss. The bunches of lavender are arranged in floral foam in an almost upright style and trimmed with a green paper tie and bow.

RIGHT

A green-painted basket of dried pink roses; a lovely way to give dried flowers as a gift. They look very attractive when they can be seen from above. Two shades of green grosgrain ribbon form a generous bow across the centre.

An impressive surround for a large mirror. The base is of dry sphagnum moss inside a tube of fine wire mesh, and it is made to the exact measurements of the mirror frame. The dried flowers are rose, lavender, larkspur, hydrangea, achillea, and cornflower, and the other components are idesia berries, acorns, (glued into their cups), nandina leaves, lichen, box leaves and trails of birch twigs with a birch twig bow as a finishing touch. The egg is glued into a hand-made bird's nest, which is wired at its precarious angle in the lower centre.

Much of this surround is arranged before the almost-complete unit is wired into place on the top of the mirror. As you are constructing it, remember to check it in its hanging place from time to time to get the perspective right.

Don't waste materials on the top back areas, which won't be seen, but allow some pieces to break the edge of the mirror frame so that the decoration doesn't look too square and rigid.

POT-POURRI

It is fun to experiment and create your own mixtures. The four pot-pourris that follow are very simple ones made by the dry method, which is the simplest way of making pot-pourri.

Buy best-quality dried flowers (or dry your own), herbs, leaves spices and oils. To create rustic mixtures, keep the ingredients as whole as possible, or, if they are in pieces, keep these large and recognisable. For instance, if you dry your own orange peel, break it into quite large pieces.

The pot-pourri containers in the photographs consist of an old battered enamel bowl, a dull tin one, an antique English china wash bowl and a well-polished pine treen bowl.

The ingredients given in the recipes are for the large amounts shown here but they can, of course, be varied. The proportions of the ingredients can be altered too; you may, for instance, prefer more marigold in the citrus pot-pourri or you might like to add some dried lemon peel. Keep a variety of shapes and textures.

You may wish to add a fixative, such as powdered orris root, to these pot-pourris. It makes the perfume long lasting, but I find it makes the mixes look dusty and I prefer just to add more oil regularly.

Stir the ingredients gently and add the oil last. I chose only one essential oil for each pot-pourri, to keep it simple. Each mixture has between 20 and 30 drops of oil, but I suggest you experiment with this to attain the strength of perfume you prefer. Don't add too much; you can always add more later, but you can't remove it.

RIGHT

ORANGE AND LEMON POT-POURRI
200 g (7 oz) orange peel
50 g (2 oz) lemon verbena leaves
25 g (1 oz) lemon grass
200 g (7 oz) rose hips
50 g (2 oz) marigold flowers
50 g (2 oz) hibiscus flowers
Bergamot essential oil

CHRISTMAS POT-POURRI
350 g (12 oz) cones (an assortment is best —
    these cones include larch, Monterey
    cypress, pine and beech nuts)
50 g (2 oz) oak moss
50 g (2 oz) nutmegs (whole)
50 g (2 oz) mace (whole)
50 g (2 oz) conifer sprigs
Patchouli essential oil

LAVENDER POT-POURRI
300 g (11 oz) lavender flowers
20 heads cornflowers
2 heads (broken down) hydrangea
8 large sprigs (broken down) rosemary
50 g (2 oz) blue malva
1 small bunch, heads only, French lavender
Lavender essential oil

SPICY BAY POT-POURRI
50 g (2 oz) bay leaves
100 g (3.5 oz) star anise
125 g (4 oz) allspice (whole)
125 g (4 oz) cardamom pods
50 g (2 oz) cloves (whole)
50 g (2 oz) linden leaves
and flowers
Cinnamon bark essential oil

CHAPTER SIX

BRINGING THE OUTDOORS INSIDE

*These Tom Thumb lettuces would look good
in the centre of a buffet table for a special
alfresco lunch.*

AN ALTERNATIVE TO DRIED MATE-rials and cut flowers are container plants. These also bring the atmosphere of the natural world into the interior of a home and, like flowers, they help to ring the changes in a room.

The plants that I mention in this chapter are more likely to be found at a garden centre than in a florist's shop. They are not the usual indoor plants; instead they are mostly inex-

FACING PAGE

Some ideas for creating an outdoor ambience: a pair of kumquat citrus trees with their small, shiny orange fruit, English lavender (Lavandula spica), a huge purple/pink kale (Brassica oleracea acephala), Tom Thumb lettuces, English box (Buxus sempervirens), violas, a pelargonium, an ivy on a topiary (Hedera helix 'Sagittaefolia variegata'), and some spring bulbs peeping through.

pensive plants that bring a country-garden feel into a home. They often cost no more than florist's flowers and, because of their longer life, are much better value. They give a 'growing' look, too, instead of an 'arranged' one, and sometimes, as a bonus, they can be planted out later.

A huge basket or preserving pan crammed with a number of yellow pansies in full bloom, will not survive for long in the corner of a dark room, but nevertheless will impart a pleasure similar to a ray of sunshine for a short while.

It is important to use a generous number of plants to create more impact, and it is best to keep to a single type and colour of plant for maximum effect.

Sometimes garden centres have trays of plants, such as marigolds or petunias, which are rather beyond their 'sell-by' date for garden use. They are in full bloom, bursting from their containers, and would be perfect indoors for a short while.

Or, if you have a garden, especially one with small plants, it is possible to first water the plant, then carefully dig it up with plenty of soil around the roots, and pot it temporarily in a suitable container for a special evening. A low bowl of flowering gentians surrounded by moss looks fabulous on a dining table. Replant it in the garden the next day. Outdoor, container-planted shrubs and trees can be brought indoors in their containers in the same way for special occasions (but remember to put a suitable water-draining receptacle underneath the pot). In pairs, large plants, such as standard flowering fuchsias, roses, bay trees, citrus trees, or trained ivies can make a great statement in a room. Put them either side of a fireplace or at each end of a sofa backed against a wall.

RIGHT

These topiaries make a bold statement in a light-filled entrance hall. Ivy has been described as the impatient topiarist's best friend; it is fast growing, is happy indoors or out, and is hardy.
The pair of topiaries on the floor have been trained on lollipop-like wire frames, spiked into the soil. The top pair are supported by pyramid-shaped wire frames.
The bird in the centre is also on a wire frame and the climber is creeping fig (Ficus pumila), a reliable vine for topiary, as it thrives in a range of temperatures and light levels.

FACING PAGE

Strawberries are the ultimate fruit: 'Doubtless God could have made a better berry, but doubtless God never did.'
(Dr William Butler)
This hanging, green-painted wire basket has been lined with moss and filled with strawberry plants. Water it and let it drain before rehanging as it will dry out quickly.

If you opt for traditional pot plants, consider buying a few quite large plants, instead of small ones dotted about a room. If you prefer small ones, group them together. Large plants make more of a statement in a room; they can also be useful for dividing an area, filling an empty space, or even creating a new one by forming a boundary. For example, in an open-plan room you could use plants to separate dining from living areas or create a conservatory feel in a corner that has good natural light.

Some of the plants that I enjoy using indoors are:

Herbs: These can grow well indoors, provided they are adequately fed and have light and air. For instant pleasure I buy small plants from a garden centre, rather than seeds. Re-pot them into attractive receptacles that suit your kitchen; they are a natural choice for the kitchen window-sill. Herbs are both ornamental and practical, and if your plants are profuse enough, sprigs can be picked for cooking, or to be included in small posies of cut flowers.

LEFT

This light, sunny kitchen makes an ideal setting for herbs. The wooden holder in the centre is a cantarera, an antique Spanish oil-pot holder. In it are two pots of American upland cress (Barbarea verna), *useful for adding interest to salads. The other herbs are parsley, applemint* (Mentha rotundifolia) *and three bay trees, two of them young standards.*

FACING PAGE

A collection of box trees (Buxus sempervirens). *The box tree makes an architectural focal point, and it is a beautiful evergreen that clips well into any shape. Box is slow growing — the trees in the photograph range in ages from one to seven years old.*

Bulbs: These look lovely grouped in a low bowl. It is more effective to plant bulbs of the same type and colour together in a bowl; different types of bulbs do not always flower at the same time. Remember that bulbs like hyacinth and narcissus, when in flower, will give a lovely fragrance to a room. If they grow tall and lanky, stake and tie them with a bold hank of raffia. Their perfume is sweet and delicious at a time when there are not many other flowers around. Buy first-grade bulbs and use them indoors in containers for just one season, then either plant them out in the garden or discard them. Large bulbs should be planted with the tips level with the surface of the potting mix, and smaller bulbs slightly under the surface. Put them in a cool, dark place to form roots; when the leaf tips have begun to show, move them to a light place, and when the tops are green move them into the sun to flower.

LEFT

A bold copper container holds a generous clump of potted Christmas lilies. They are still in their plastic pots inside the container, with a covering of fresh green moss. The natural paper tie and bow add a finishing touch. These plants will last much longer than cut lilies, and they have buds still waiting to come out.

FACING PAGE

Some container ideas for geraniums: an old, chipped, blue enamel wash-bowl, a white enamel bucket and a yellow china chamber pot. The plants we call geraniums are botanically Pelargoniums; *they are old and reliable favourites, with a vast colour range. They have attractive leaves and some are scented.*

Primulas and pansies: Wide, shallow baskets look lovely when massed with these flowers. Choose plants with plenty of buds.

FACING PAGE

A two-sided, wooden, antique cutlery box makes an interesting holder for these velvety, rusty red pansies. The box is lined with heavy black polythene, which does not allow for drainage, so one must be careful not to over-water the plants.

ABOVE

Single gerberas in a mix of vibrant colours are set in a heavy copper pan. The gerberas are left in their plastic pots, which do not show because of the profuse leaf growth at their bases.

Kale (Brassica oleracea acephala): Ornamental kale (from the cabbage family) is an unusual decorative plant, which can be variegated white or purple/pink. A mass of plants can look striking in a tin bath, or planted individually in pots and placed in pairs.

Interesting containers can transform plants. With the addition of a plastic liner or plastic saucer in the bottom, before you insert the plant, wooden barrels, copper preserving pans, baskets of many shapes and sizes, and wooden boxes can become a focal point in a room.

RIGHT

This fresh green French cache-pot is packed with planted, acid-yellow marigolds (Tagetes).

FACING PAGE

A battered, rusted old preserving pan, with lots of character, holds these capsicums. They make attractive ornamental plants, but they do need regular watering.

CHAPTER SEVEN

BEHIND THE SCENES

Some of the tools of the trade: secateurs, stub wire and silver reel wire, knives, sticks of glue, wooden spoon, large needle and twine, rubber bands, and a small hammer.

CHOOSING CONTAINERS

Country-style flower arrangements lend themselves to unusual containers. It can be more a matter of initiative than of great financial outlay. Church fêtes, white elephant stalls, junk shops, country fairs, markets and auctions are all good places to look for inexpensive, interesting items.

As a rule I select plain containers of simple shape and natural colours. These are the safest, and unpatterned surfaces don't detract from the flowers. Learn to size up likely items

FACING PAGE

Baskets, antique and new, tin pans, a cast-iron boiler, a wooden barrel and trug, straw, willow and vine wreaths, clay pots and jugs: these are just some ideas for containers and bases with which to create country-style flower arrangements.

by picturing them away from their immediate environment. Envisage them filled with flowers or foliage, in your own surroundings. Remember how useful paint, especially with a decorative finish, can be to transform a surface.

Metal containers such as old galvanised buckets, watering cans and baths (there are also modern copies of all the old tin vessels) go well with silver and grey foliages, and blue to purple and dusky pink flowers. Pewter also enhances these colours. Look out for lovely old pewter mugs, measures and jugs.

Copper and brass lend themselves to autumn tonings. Keep a look-out for preserving pans, saucepans, moulds, and cider measures. Enamel, even with chips out of it, looks great in a kitchen.

Wire, too, has been used to make attractive containers. The one on page 33 is a Victorian rubbish basket and the slightly battered small mesh container with the wire handle on page 86 has lots of character. Both are lined with greyish green mosses. A wire egg basket could be lined with straw and a plastic bowl.

Small, stoneware mustard, honey, Stilton cheese or marmalade pots are charming for small, compact bunches of one type of flower, or little garden mixtures. Large stoneware jars, too, are good for bold mixtures. Old or good reproduction tin cannisters are also interesting. Wooden cutlery boxes and bread bins can be used with a liner. Look in antique shops or junk shops and stalls for china soup tureens, vegetable dishes, jugs and old jelly moulds.

Small, old jugs and vases painted with mixed flowers can look charming with colourful mixtures of simple flowers.

There are masses of beautiful baskets available, old and new, and they are wonderful for creating a simple country look. Because they are handmade they tend to have a look of the past. Cane, rattan, vine, roots — all make good baskets. A very attractive example is the English Sussex trug made of willow strips, which gives arranged flowers a soft, low, flowing look (see page 68). The finely crafted Shaker baskets and boxes also make good containers.

Weave some moss into your basket if you want to create a ragged look. I sometimes tangle bare birch or tortured willow twigs around the handle or rim of a basket as well, to make it extra ragged (page 122).

Old baskets, with the patina of age, are full of character. Displayed with flowers, or empty, they make a simple decoration.

Baskets need waterproof liners. As they will not be seen it does not matter what they look like. Many kitchen items are suitable — mixing bowls, salad bowls, pie dishes and baking tins. Plastic ice cream, yoghurt or honey pottles, take-away food dishes (as long as the plastic is not too flimsy) are all suitable to save up for later use. Vessels that will rust, like old metal cake tins, need to be treated to prevent rusting.

You can line a basket with heavy polythene and use wet floral foam to hold your arrangement. Polythene is also suitable for a vessel lining for plants; but do not make the mistake of using polythene if you are using crumpled wire for fresh flowers, as it can get punctured and cause a flood.

If your basket is an open-weave one, you may need to use brown paper or a liner in a neutral colour, so that you do not see the liner through the weave.

Wooden bowls, troughs, cheese presses, grain sieves and bread bins all make interesting holders for plants or flowers. Wine, fruit and tea boxes are good for dried arrangements or plants. The classic Versailles tub can take on a 'country' look with the right contents and accessories. I picked up a battered, two-compartment tool-box washed up on a beach — it had probably fallen off a boat — and now, planted with herbs, it gives me great pleasure (page 114). The wooden slatted basket on page 42 is lined with dry straw and has an ice cream container holding the wire and water.

The Welsh potato basket on page 8 has an interesting wire bottom; I lined it with a roasting pan.

The lovely reproduction 18th-century specimen vase on page 44 has a pretty garden mixture. You may like to imitate this idea with glass chemistry test tubes in a wooden rack.

PREPARING FOR
AN ARRANGEMENT

Flower arranging should not be rule-bound. Learn to develop an eye for what is pleasing and, with confidence, you can develop a natural instinct for what looks right. To create a country look, let a natural appearance and simplicity be your guide, but make sure that the flower size and height are correct for the scale of your container.

Visualise what the finished arrangement will look like before you start so that you have a plan to follow.

If picking flowers from the garden, choose stems that will suit the vase — curving in different directions — and try not to pick more than you need. Experience is really the only thing that will teach you how much to pick for your container.

Pick some buds; they are useful as a light outline and often have a lovely form. As an alternative to buds, pick some small-headed flowers and lighter foliage for the outline. Pick the stems as long as you can (without causing undue damage to the plant), so that you can choose where to place them in the arrangement. They can be cut down, if necessary, when you come to use them.

Commercially grown flowers are usually straight stemmed and perfect. But nature never intended roses to have straight stems one metre long! Think about buying or picking bent stems, which are often considered second grade or deformed. They may be just what you need to give soft edges and sculptural outlines to an arrangement, instead of a straight, upright, surprised look.

Sometimes second-grade flowers are better because they are smaller; flowers such as lilies, with a mass of large heads on one stem, can be difficult to arrange because they are so large. One huge cluster might be ideal for the centre of an arrangement, but for the outline it would look heavy (unless your arrangement was a huge one, for a special occasion). Fewer blooms on the end of a stem are more suitable for an outline.

Remember, too, flowers that you buy are often all at the same stage of opening, so that you don't achieve the natural look that you would with a few buds, a few partly open blooms and some fully open flowers. People without a garden source can still achieve this 'gardeny' feel, with a few leaves picked at random.

It is useful to grow foliages to supplement bought flowers, as it is these, and other materials, that give your arrangement a soft, casual, country look. I can never find enough interesting foliages; flower markets and shops seem to be restricted to supplying the same boring greenery.

I use 5 cm, 20-gauge mesh wire netting as the support in most of my arrangements. It can be galvanised or plastic coated. I find that flowers do not last as well in floral foam and it is costly. However, it is useful for arrangements which must be portable, and for occasions when I am doing a number of arrangements and speed is vital. I also use it for displays that I want to suspend or show at awkward angles for special occasions. Floral foam is quite good for a beginner to use, as the stems will stay exactly where they are put, but it is better to try to progress to wire, as you will achieve a more soft, country look.

Foam is also useful for many dried arrangements — the upright 'hedge' look is easy to achieve with it, and a dried arrangement usually remains in place for longer than a fresh one.

Foam can be secured to a vase by pressing it on to a florist's spike, which is attached to the bottom of the vase with adhesive clay. Or it can be tied in like wire netting.

The correct wiring of your container is one of the most important details of your floral arrangement. (See the step-by-step illustrations on pages 164-168.) Cut a square of wire mesh to suit the vase you are using — practice is really the only way to learn to judge how much wire is needed for the size of the vase. Roll the wire lightly from corner to corner, lightly fold in the ends and push the mass into your container. Ease the layers apart so that they are evenly distributed. Allow the top level to rise a little above the level of the container; this allows some stems to be placed almost horizontally if they have a curved end, and they can still reach the water level. Tie the whole container and mesh like a parcel with wire or fine string.

Alternatively, drill four holes into the rim of your liner. Then you can thread the wire or string through the holes, loop it over at the centre, and create a very secure base.

Containers with strong handles at the top, or those made from wire or cane mesh, also provide good anchors to tie the wire or string around.

You may choose to use a pinholder in the bottom of your container as well as wire, in which case the holder would have to be placed in the container first.

Before begining, fill the vase with tepid water almost to the top, leaving a little room to top up later and to allow space for the stems. Once the vase is arranged it is difficult to judge the correct amount of water to put in. Some flowers will also wilt if you take a long time to arrange them without water and their stem tips dry out, making it hard for them to take up water. Make sure your vase does not leak and that its bottom is dry.

It is preferable to put your vase in the place where it is going to stand — especially if it is large and/or heavy. The scale of your arrangement is more likely to be right, too. If you are not arranging it *in situ*, try to do it on an equivalent level.

Make sure the container is level and secure and, if it has features like handles, that they are in the correct position. Do not use containers that are too light to hold flowers; remember, though, that the water will add to the weight. Stones or lead pieces on the bottom of a light container also help.

Some containers are so large that they would not be moveable when full of water, so have a watering can handy if you are going to have to carry water to the container.

BASIC RULES
FOR ARRANGING FLOWERS

The following rules apply to the country-style (mostly fresh) arrangements in this book.

Begin the arrangement with your outline of either light flowers or foliage (see the step-by-step details on page 166). Ensure that the outline is stable, as it is annoying to have important outline stems swivel round when you are half-way through your arrangement. You may need to rearrange sections of the wire mesh so that they clasp the major stems. As you progress, the stems themselves will help to support each other. But, like the correct wiring of your container, the initial few outline stems are important.

If you place your choice, central flowers or any delicate blooms before you are near the end of your arrangement, they will get damaged as you try to work around them. You may like to put them in, to envisage what the end result will look like, then remove them

before you continue with the arrangement.

Try not to have a flat back to a facing arrangement: allow some stems to lean back and break the line.

It is more pleasing to the eye to see odd numbers of a few choice blooms. Four dominant blooms often look like a square or triangle, whereas three or five look better. But in the case of one or two full-blown garden roses, or other special blooms, place them centrally, quite close together.

Place the centre-back stems three-quarters of the way back in the container for a facing arrangement. The reason for this is that if the stems started at the back of the container, you would end up with a massive amount of flowers in the centre and out over the front rim, giving a rather bulged effect. Make sure there are some backward-leaning stems. When the arrangement is complete, pop a few stems of greenery into the back to cover the mechanics.

As a general rule, the height of your arrangement should be one-and-a-half to two times the height of your container. Arrange some outline branches softly over the lower edge at the sides and front to break any straight line that may occur at the base of the arrangement. If you have any curved, light pieces, these are ideal here. Breaking the line also helps the vase and contents appear as one unit rather than separate parts.

Distribute flowers of one type gracefully through your arrangement. Or, in the case of one type of small flower, like a bunch of lavender, pop it in as a clump rather than dotting it about (see page 124).

Step back from the arrangement from time to time for an overall view. Look at it from the side also if it will be seen from that angle. If it is for a dining table where people will be seated, check that the height is correct and that it won't interfere with the guests' vision.

OTHER POINTS TO REMEMBER
- No stems which are side by side should be of the same length.
- The width of the arrangement generally is about the same as the height.

- Build your arrangement from the outside, working inwards.
- Cut some flowers short to create depth.
- Make sure that when viewed from the side, the arrangement doesn't look flat.

Use three or five large leaves (like hosta) to visually pull the centre of the arrangement together. They also form a background for special central blooms or fruit and sometimes have the added bonus of covering the mechanics.

A round arrangement (to be seen from all sides) should have its outline placed in first. If it is for a table centre, it is usually more pleasing for its outline to almost touch the surface of the table. This is also important if you want to disguise the container if you are using unattractive plastic containers. Be careful, though, not to put stems at such an angle that they syphon water out of the vase and ruin a table top. As with front-facing arrangements, place some flowers facing sideways, so that they don't all look to the front, or top, like soldiers. The stems should all appear to radiate from the centre, like most growing plants.

FRUIT PYRAMID FROM PAGE 19

On the stand is placed a cone shape cut from dry floral foam, with ivy leaves peeping from underneath it around the edge. The fruit at the base does not need to be anchored, as it rests on the tazza edge, but as you put pieces in place, moving up the pyramid, you will need to use 'staples' of bent wire for things like the small bunches of grapes, the unripe spindleberries and the elderberries. Place small items at the top and large items at the base for a balanced look. Toothpicks are used for the blackberries and the huge plums that are at a higher level. (Satay sticks could be used for the larger fruit, too.) Fresh flowers could be included in this display. If you wish to do so, use a cone of wet floral foam to spike the stems into. You may also need to use staples of florist's wire to secure the flowers near the surface of the cone; the secret is to keep the components close and compact, as it is quite a formal topiary shape.

MAKING DRIED TOPIARIES

Purchase round balls of dry floral foam. For small, light topiaries you will need an extra piece that can be cut to fit inside the containers. The stems here are large sticks of cinnamon bark, but you could use bamboo or wooden twigs. The other materials are natural-coloured reindeer moss, artificial crab-apples and larger fruit (these are easy to use because they already have wire stems that can be cut to length), wooden apples and pears, and orange ribbon. For the stems of the large topiaries shown on page 134, cylinders made out of paper-covered, heavy cardboard have been used, but thick branches are another alternative.

To set up a topiary, spike the stem into the foam ball in the centre, and dribble some glue around it to make it secure. Now spike the

stem into the base, also in the centre, with glue dribbled around it as well. Do this at the beginning, otherwise, if you try to attach the topiaries to their stems after they have been completed, they may be damaged. As with any arrangement, it is very important to take great care with the initial preparation, so that the topiary does not collapse half-way through, or, worse still, when it is in place.

Terracotta pots make good containers for topiaries. If you are using these, put a small piece of cardboard over the holes in the bottom of the pots, as the foam is gritty and grains drop through the holes. Cut some chunks of floral foam to fit tightly into your pots, as shown above. The topiaries on page 104 have been glued directly on to the clay pots.

Large, heavy topiaries (such as those on

page 134) require a heavier base than foam. The stems for these are set in plaster of Paris in small plastic buckets. (Make sure the buckets fit inside your container first.) By setting the stems in buckets, it means that these urns can be used at a later date for some other arrangement. If you want to put plaster directly into your container — say a flower-pot — remember that plaster expands when it is drying, so you need to slip some strips of corrugated cardboard or floral foam down inside the sides of your container to allow for expansion. Do this before you begin: plaster sets very quickly, and you won't have time to search around for cardboard or suchlike once you've poured the wet plaster into your container.

If you follow this process you will have very stable bases on which to work and you are therefore not likely to have items falling apart when you are in the middle of an elaborate piece.

When you decorate your topiary, put in the biggest items first, as they need to be evenly distributed. This is also important for other items, but the large ones are particularly obvious if they are uneven. Depending on their weight, you may need a dab of glue at the base even if they do have wire stems.

Make small 'staples' of light gauge wire, and use them to anchor in clumps of moss and ribbons.

The materials in the topiaries on the facing page are natural-coloured reindeer moss, artificial crab-apples and larger fruit (these are easy to use because they already have wire stems that can be cut to length), wooden apples and pears, and orange ribbon. Cut the ribbon into short lengths, but make sure they are long enough to show their tips when pressed in beside the biggest item.

Some moss should separate each item. The wooden fruits that have no stem are fixed in place with a generous amount of glue (but not so much that it is visible), and moss is stapled around the base to cover the foam.

The completed topiaries are on pages 60, 104, 105, 134 and 139.

MAKING A SIMPLE WREATH

The large wreath on page 107 was made from a base of grape vine twisted into a circle, but you could buy a base. Bare branches of larch, with a few cones still attached, are tangled in and out of the vine; they could be wired in places, but this should not be necessary.

Long-lasting conifer (in this case *Cedrus deodara* (Indian cedar) and *Cupressus glabra*) branches are also tangled into the vine. Small sticks with cones still firmly attached are either glued on to the vine (not the greenery) at intervals around the wreath, or they can be wired as in the photograph. Larger cones are wired in clusters of three at intervals around the wreath, but they also could be glued.

Three large ivy leaves are glued underneath each cluster of cones. The ivy leaves will not last, but they can easily be replaced without disturbing the wreath.

The rough country look of this wreath means that materials can be placed in it quite casually, but I think it is more pleasing to the eye if all the branches face in the same direction.

STEPS FOR A SIMPLE
FRONT-FACING ARRANGEMENT

STEP ONE: All flowers and foliage have been treated and immersed in water for some time. The container to be used is a wire mesh basket that will hold a plastic bowl for water. A piece of 5 cm wire mesh has been cut in a square shape, measuring about 45 cm x 45 cm.

STEP TWO: The basket is lined with moss to disguise the plastic bowl. The moss also gives a rustic appearance and shows up the old wire mesh of the basket.

The piece of wire mesh is rolled from corner to corner as described in the text on page 161. The wire mesh is placed in the bowl, which has tiny holes drilled very near the top rim, and reel wire is passed through these and over the wire mesh like a parcel. (If the bowl did not have holes drilled in it, I would put it into the basket and then secure the wire through the top rim of the basket.)

STEP THREE: The bowl is now secure in the basket. Three-quarters fill the bowl with warm water and put the first stems in place. Here I have used quite a few pieces of foliage as outline pieces and have followed the rules as described in the text on page 161.

I have placed only two roses ('Chantilly Lace') in the outline — I have only 10 roses in total and want to keep enough to appear right through the finished arrangement. I have also used the more closed roses on the outline and kept the fuller blooms for nearer the centre.

STEP FOUR: Most of the stems are now in place, except for the centre. Passionfruit have been spiked with satay sticks and a bunch of grapes has been cut into smaller, lighter bunches. The grapes have been wired and the wire stem formed into a hook to loop over the mesh in the bowl.

STEP FIVE: The arrangement is complete.
Three large hosta leaves are placed around the
three central roses, and the fruit is clustered
as a focal point.
  Now top up the bowl with water.

CHAPTER EIGHT

TIPS ON CARE

Treated and untreated stems: a freshly picked rose, and one which has been de-thorned, had the lower leaves removed, the stem cut at an angle and split; a hammered eucalyptus stem; sedum stems, one of which has been split and had its lower leaves removed, ready to go into warm water.

CUT FLOWERS FROM THE GARDEN either in the early morning or early evening when they are at their peak condition.

If stems are not put into water as soon as they are picked, they should be re-cut, as the stem tips will have dried out and will not take up water readily.

Romantic baskets to lay flowers in may look beautiful but are not practical, as the flowers are likely to dry out and may also damage one another.

Flowers picked in bud will obviously last longer than fully open flowers. However, you may have a fully blown rose which you can't resist picking — and it's worth it, even for a day's pleasure.

Be careful not to pick buds that are too tightly closed. They may never open, or may open into puny little specimens. If flowers are not picked at the correct stage of growth, nothing will keep them alive for very long.

Avoid cutting a bloom with lots of surrounding, underdeveloped buds that will flower later if left on the plant.

GENERAL HINTS FOR THE CARE OF FLOWERS

- Cut the stems — don't pull stems off plants, as this causes damage.
- Split or crush woody stems.
- Use good-quality, sharp cutters so that stems are cut cleanly and do not look 'chewed'.
- Cut stems at an angle. It gives the stem a larger area through which to drink and also means that the stem cannot seal on to the bottom of the container.

- Remove any bottom leaves which will be below the water level, but do not strip the stalks completely — leave the flowers looking as natural as possible.
- Have plenty of clean buckets, filled with fresh, clean, tepid tap water and a cool place in which to stand them.
- Put small flowers in small containers.
- Keep only a few flowers to a bucket.
- Do not force petals open.
- Don't arrange flowers in draughts.
- Stand the flowers in a bucket of water, preferably overnight, in a cool place, before arranging them.
- Do not put flowers in a household refrigerator — it is too cold.
- If possible, change the water in your vase every one or two days.

You may wish to use some of the proprietary substances that extend the life of cut flowers. Or use a few drops of bleach in the water, especially if the flowers are of the type that develops smelly stems (such as stock).

Flowers offered for sale on the street or in open markets are likely to have deteriorated in the weather more than those from a shop (which may have a cooler), but they are also likely to be less expensive.

If flowers flag after they have been arranged, pull them out of the arrangement and repeat the care process.

STEM CARE

Hard, woody stems, e.g. rhododendron, lilac, fruit-tree blossom, foliage. Scrape the outer bark with a sharp knife for about 4 cm up the stem, and cut the end at a slant. Hammer the end (using a wooden mallet on a tree trunk is a good idea). Strip off the bottom leaves.

Thick fleshy stems, e.g. hyacinth, narcissus. Cut the stem at an angle, and discard the white part of the stem. Flowers like narcissus, which exude a slimy sap, should be cut and placed in water on their own for a few hours until the sap has gone. They then should be arranged in fresh water.

Stems that bleed, e.g. poppy, euphorbia, poinsettia, some dahlias. Seal the tips for 15 seconds in boiling water (protect the flower heads from the steam) or in a flame, then put them into warm water. If any side sprigs are removed, seal them with a lighted match or gas lighter.

Hollow stems, e.g. lupin, delphinium, large dahlia, amaryllis, hollyhock. Push a split bamboo cane or thin stick up the hollow stem to stop it from bending. Invert the stem, fill it with tepid water, plug it with tissue and bind it in place with a rubber band. Place it in a deep bucket of tepid water.

EXTRA HINTS

Roses: The longer the stem, the more difficult these can be to keep. Remove the thorns and lower leaves. Cut the stems at an angle and split them for a short way. Place them in deep water. If they show signs of flagging, re-cut them, lay them on a piece of paper with their heads all facing upwards, roll them up firmly and place the cylinder shape in deep, warm water for at least two hours. The stems will become strong and upright again.

Carnations: Cut the stems between the leaf areas. If the two white stamens are exposed, the centre of the bloom is soft to touch, and the petal tips curl inwards, they are not fresh.

Poppies: Buy them in bud, as they open quickly. Seal the tips as described above (stems that bleed).

Lilies: With your fingers, remove pollen from the flowers. Remove the lower leaves, cut the stems at an angle, and stand them in warm water.

Hydrangeas: Immerse the flower heads in cold water for an hour. To freshen up limp, new blooms, cut the stems, split them and stand the flowers in water in a cool place.

Violets: Immerse both flower heads and stems in cold water.

Narcissi, tulips, irises, lilies: Buy them in bud and treat as above.

Daisy-type flowers: Such as single-spray chrysanthemums, should have a hard, green centre with a small ring of pollen at the petal base. If the centre is yellow and covered in pollen, it means that the flowering is partly over.

Gladioli: Nip out the buds at the tip. This encourages the flowers to come out.

ACKNOWLEDGEMENTS

My special thanks go to Dianne Molloy, whose interest in the country theme and personal encouragement have been invaluable.

I should also like to thank Mr David Steen, who allowed me access to his beautiful garden, and the following people: Shirley Anderson, Jane Cennamo, Faye Chandler, Lea and Robert Chapman, Christine Fernyhough, Virginia Fisher, Fleur Hill, Rhys and Terry Hitchcock, Hannah Holm, Queenie Lagoutaris, Joanna Masfen, the Peebles family, Sharon Prichard, Susan Rhodes, Rita Salmon, Rosie Schneideman, and Cathy Veninga.

I am also grateful to Gary Armiger, Juliet Bamford, Jetta and Bruce Cornish, Chris Fleming, Lynley and Malcolm Grover, Alan Gundersen, Graham Hart, Raymond and Daniel Hill, Viki Miller, Dorothy Motoi, Peter Ross, Jo Seagar, Jo Stewart, Craig Thorburn, Paul and Gordon Verdon and Sonia Watts.

Special thanks must also go to Donna Hoyle, Nick Tresidder and Diana Harris, whose creativity and flair have been an eye-opener to a first-time author; and to Martin Keay who helped me with identification of plants.

INDEX